365 Drawing Prompts

AN IDEA FOR EACH DAY OF THE YEAR!

Improve your skills and grow your portfolio by drawing something different each day of the year.
Let these 365 prompts spark your imagination and draw whatever comes to mind!
You decide if your drawing will be large or small, realistic or abstract, simple or detailed.
It's all up to you!
The possibilities are endless when it comes to art, perspective, and interpretation!
Have fun!

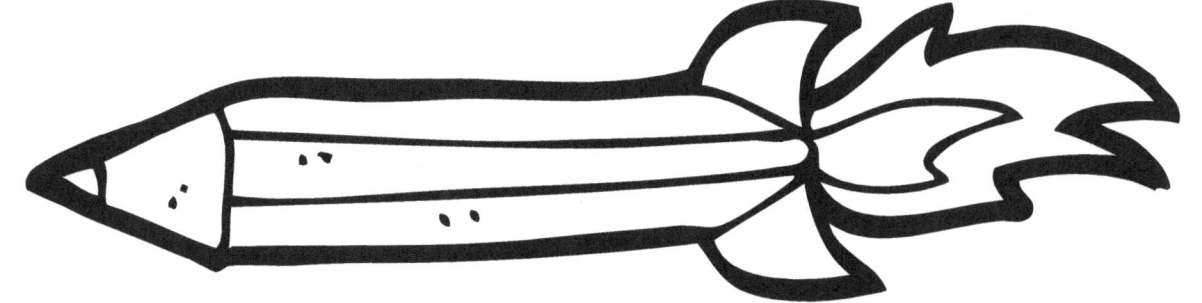

1. Cube
2. Sphere
3. Pyramid
4. Cone
5. Wedge
6. Hallway
7. Staircase
8. Ladder
9. Winding Road
10. Rearview Mirror

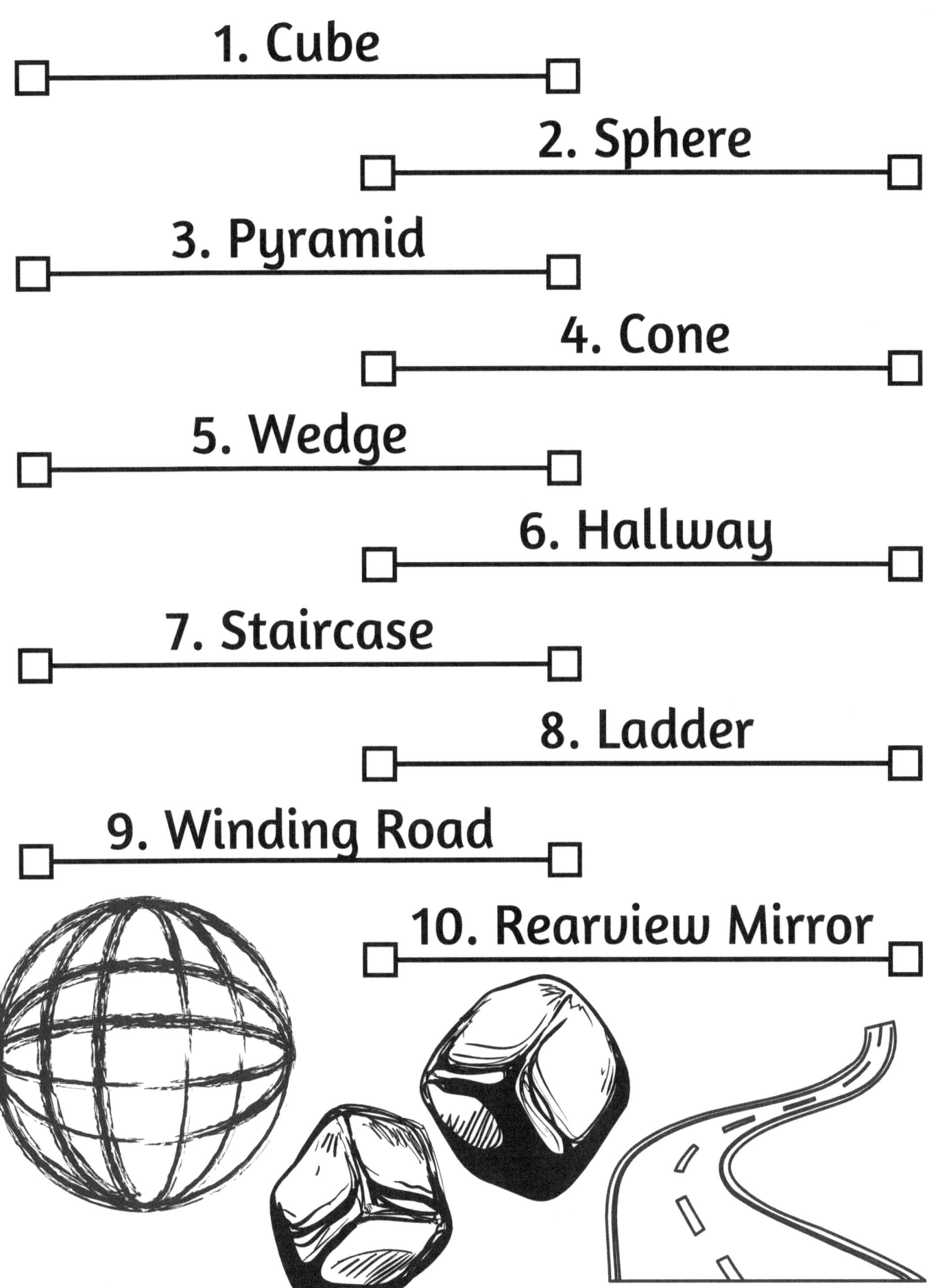

☐———— 11. Eyes ————☐

☐———— 12. Nose ————☐

☐———— 13. Ear ————☐

☐———— 14. Mouth ————☐

☐———— 15. Feet ————☐

☐———— 16. Hands ————☐

☐———— 17. Straight Hair ————☐

☐———— 18. Curly Hair ————☐

☐———— 19. Short, spiky hair ————☐

☐———— 20. Face ————☐

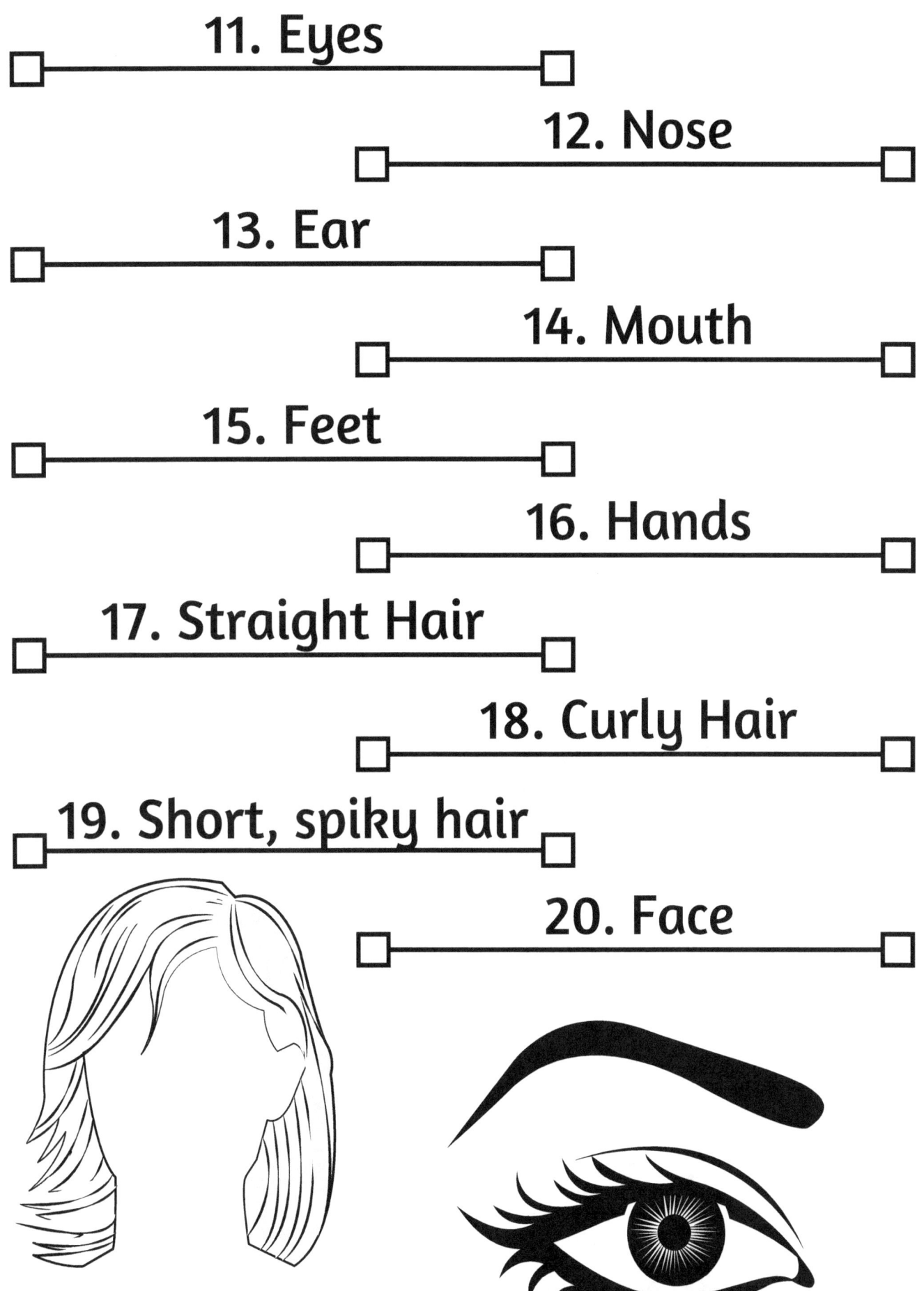

21. Dog
22. Cat
23. Monkey
24. Elephant
25. Owl
26. Penguin
27. Bear
28. Horse
29. Mouse
30. Lion

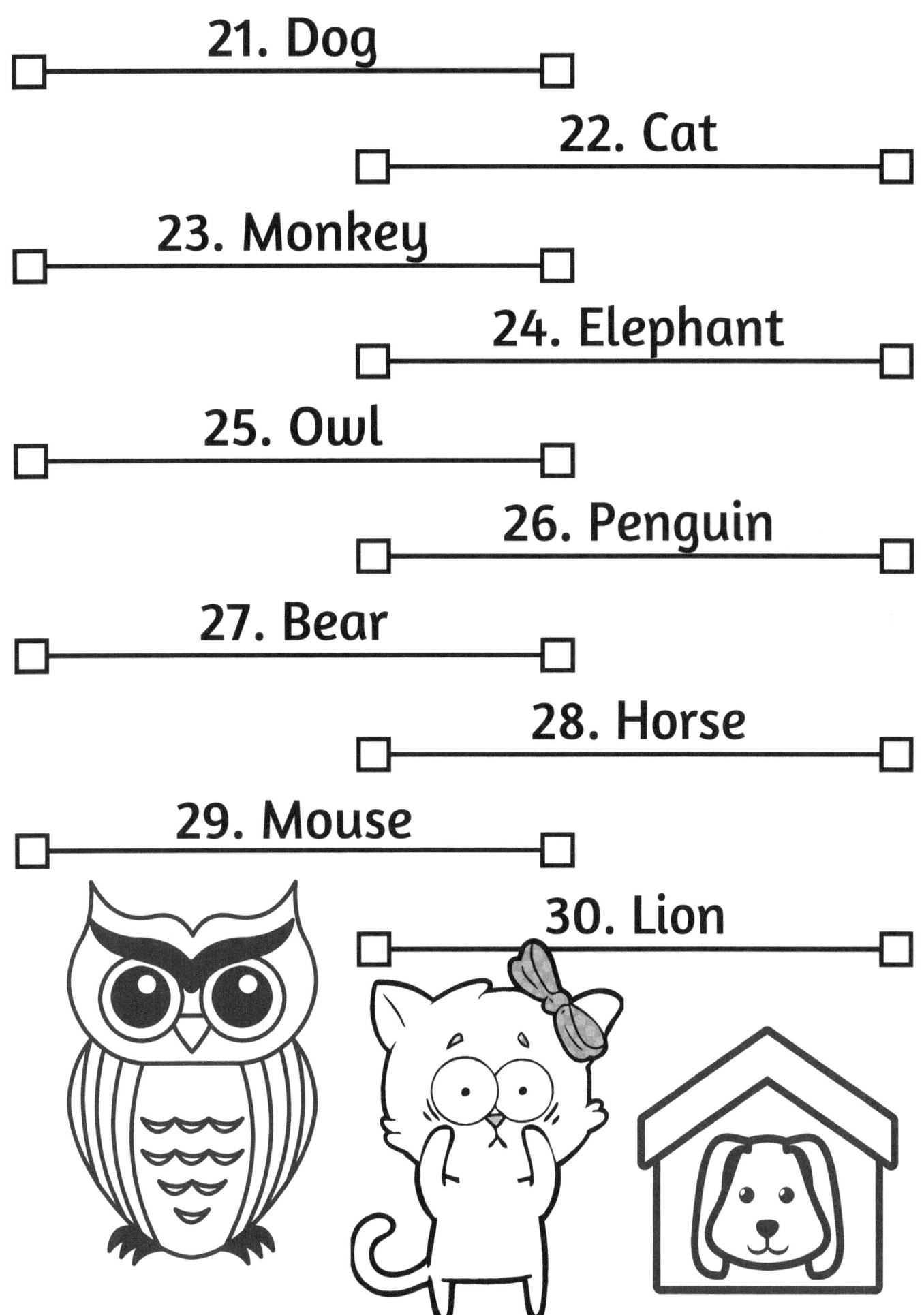

☐——— 31. Vampire ———☐

☐——— 32. Werewolf ———☐

☐——— 33. Witch ———☐

☐——— 34. Wizard ———☐

☐——— 35. Mermaid ———☐

☐——— 36. Fairy ———☐

☐——— 37. Wand ———☐

☐——— 38. Book of Spells ———☐

☐——— 39. Cauldron ———☐

☐——— 40. Ghost ———☐

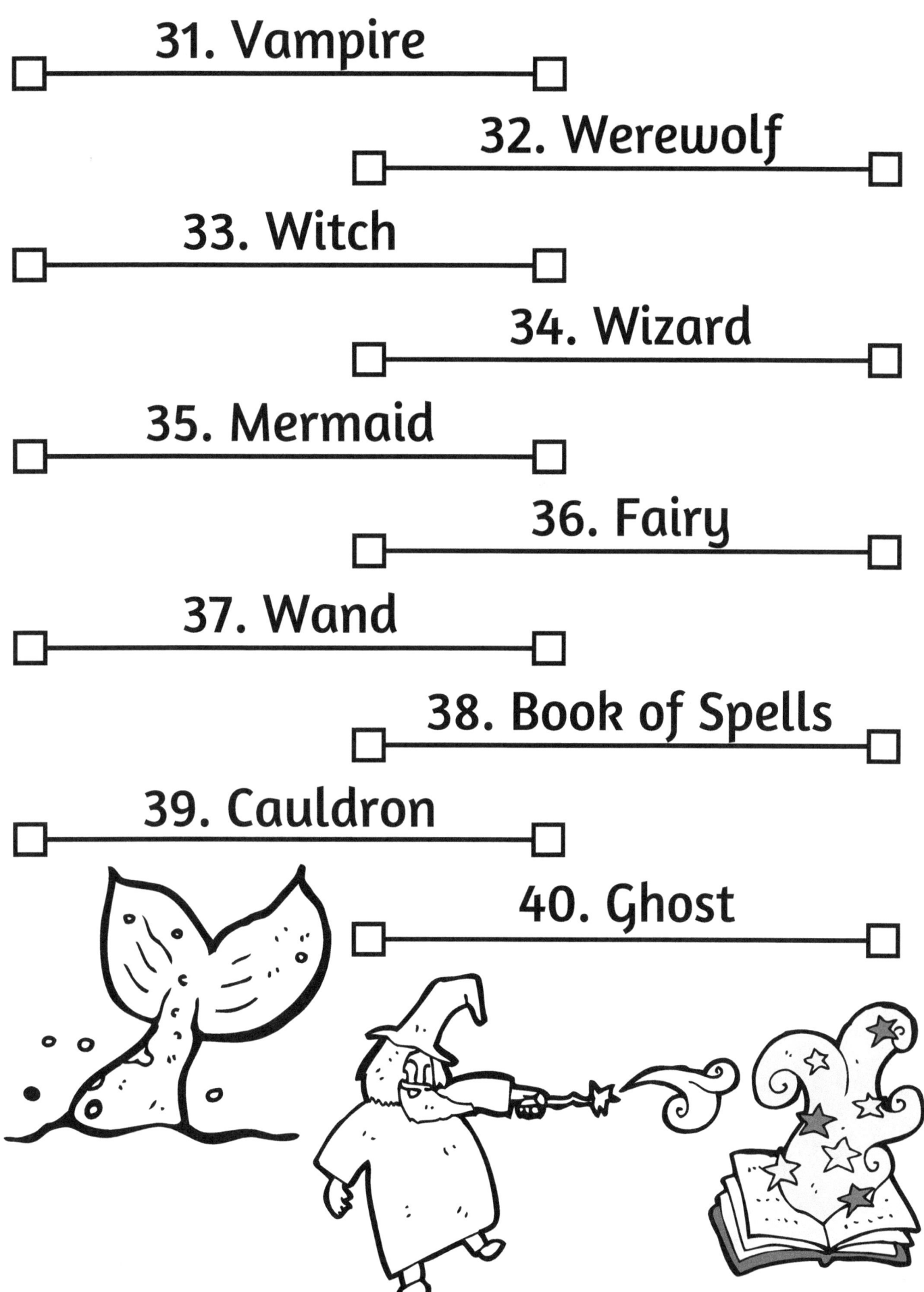

41. Car

42. Truck

43. Van

44. Firetruck

45. Ambulance

46. Tractor

47. Motorcycle

48. Scooter

49. Convertible

50. R-V

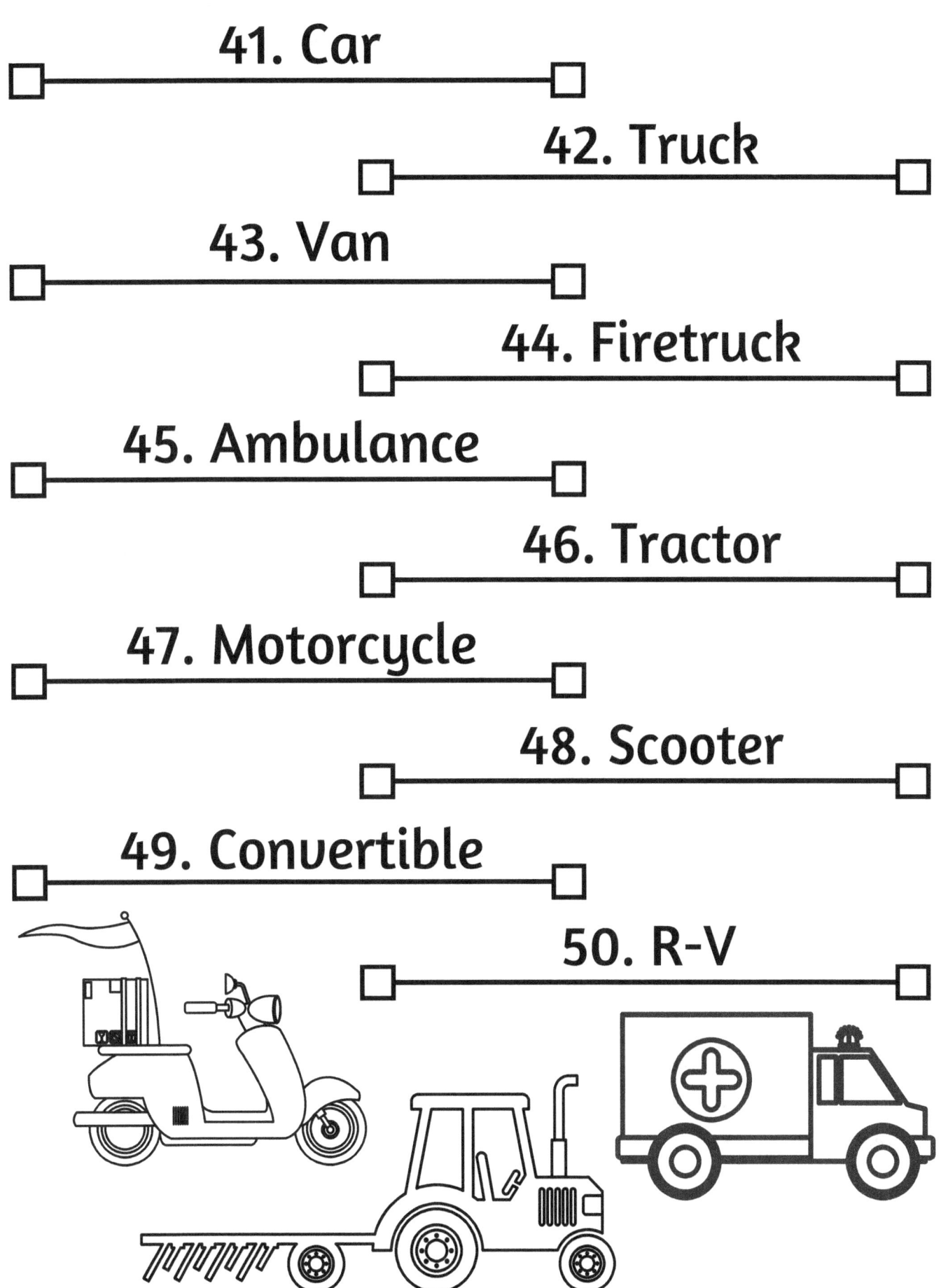

51. Train

52. Airplane

53. Helicopter

54. Speed Boat

55. Jet Ski

56. Skateboard

57. Canoe

58. Kayak

59. Sailboat

60. Bicycle

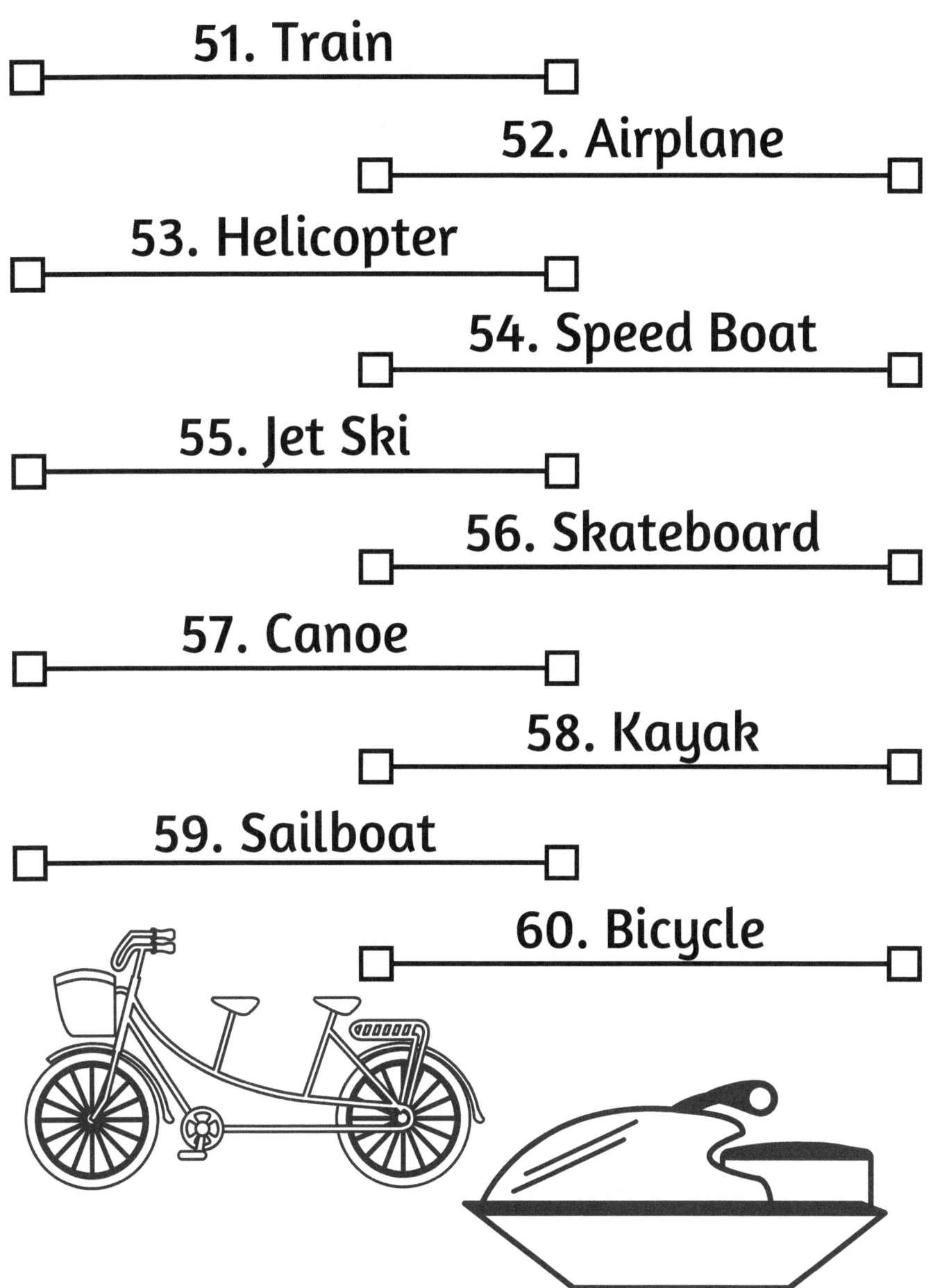

61. Football

62. Basketball

63. Soccer

64. Baseball

65. Volleyball

66. Golf

67. Tennis

68. Bowling

69. Hockey

70. Archery

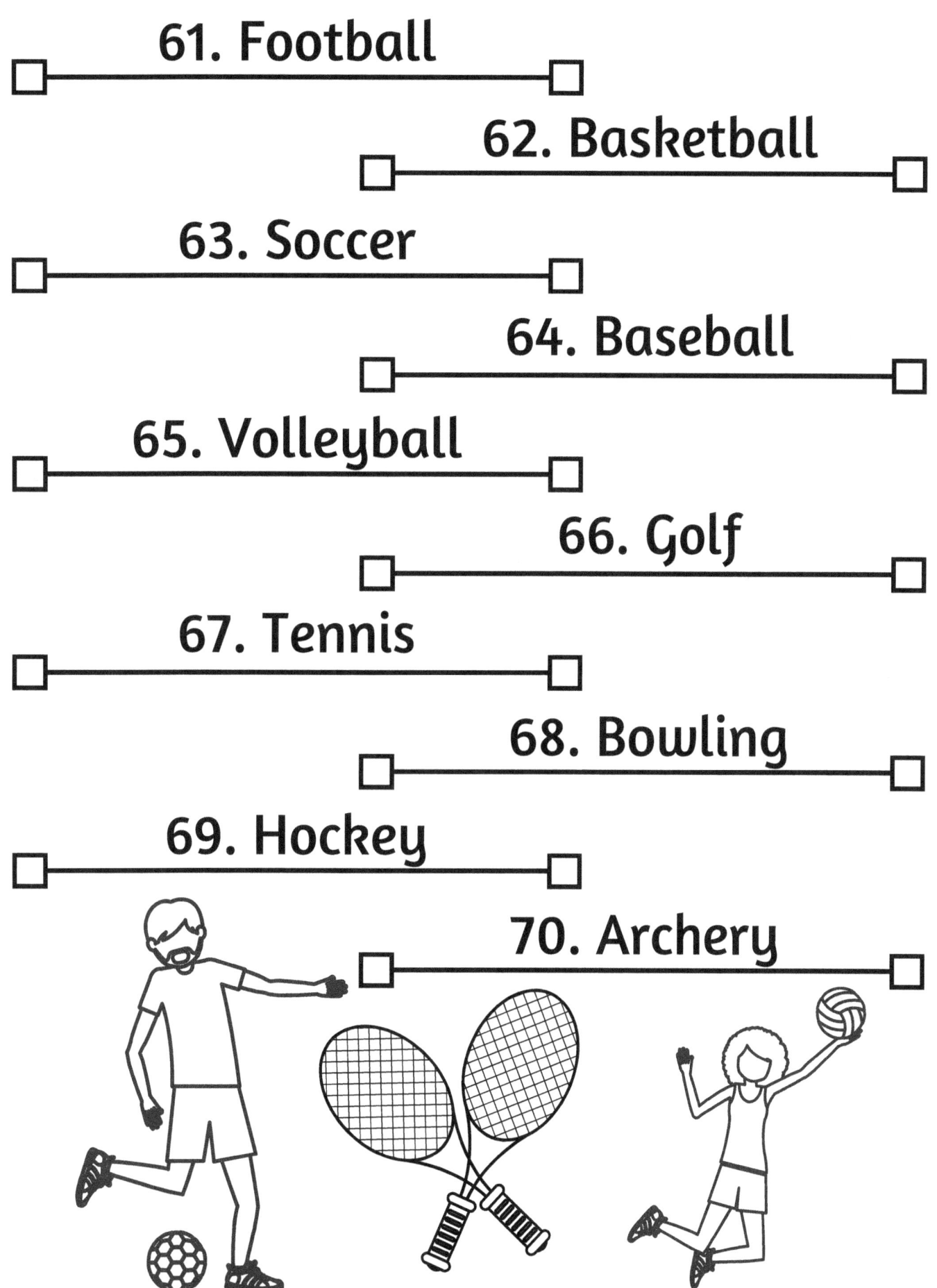

71. Ice Skating

72. Skiing

73. Surfing

74. Water Ski

75. Fishing

76. Hunting

77. Gymnastics

78. Billiards

79. Boxing

80. Wrestling

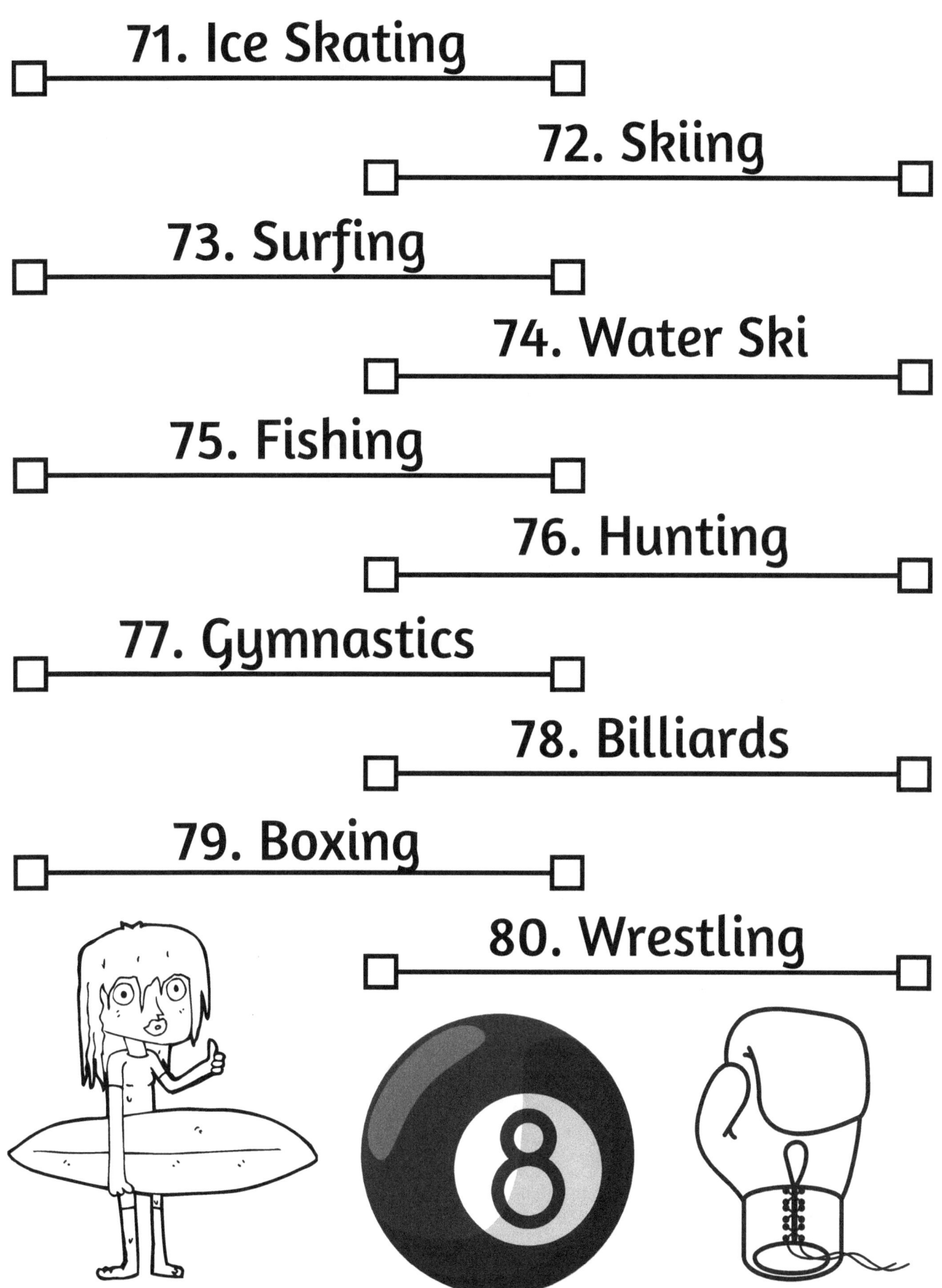

81. Lunges

82. Dumbells

83. Barbell

84. Bench Press

85. Jump Rope

86. Running

87. Scale

88. Treadmill

89. Swimming

90. Pushups

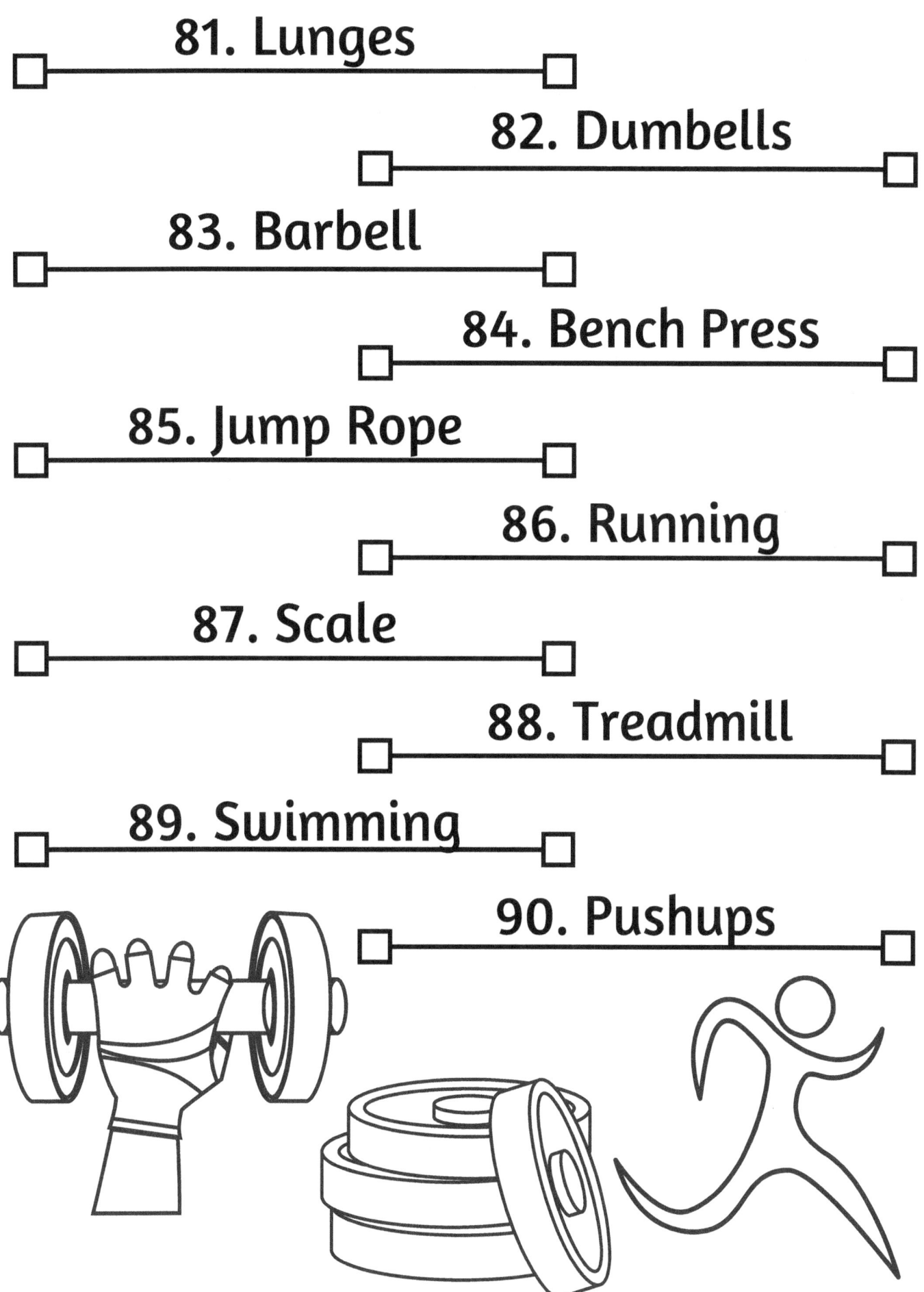

91. Chess
92. Card Games
93. Puzzles
94. Checkers
95. Tetherbal
96. Monkey Bars
97. Tic-Tac-Toe
98. Playground
99. Classroom
100. Bell

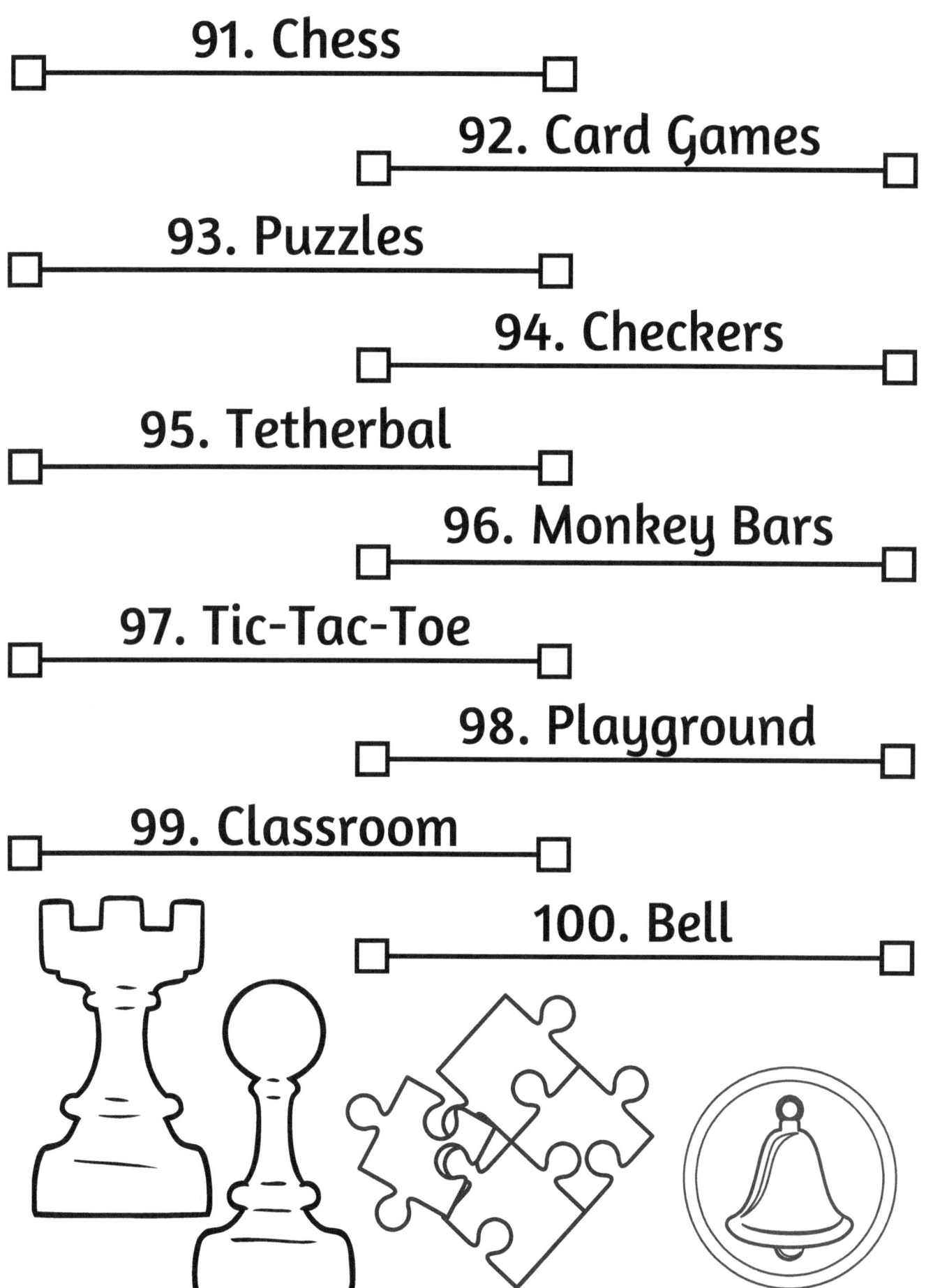

101. School

102. House

103. Church

104. Bank

105. Supermarket

106. Skyscraper

107. Cabin

108. Theatre

109. Auto Shop

110. Floorplan

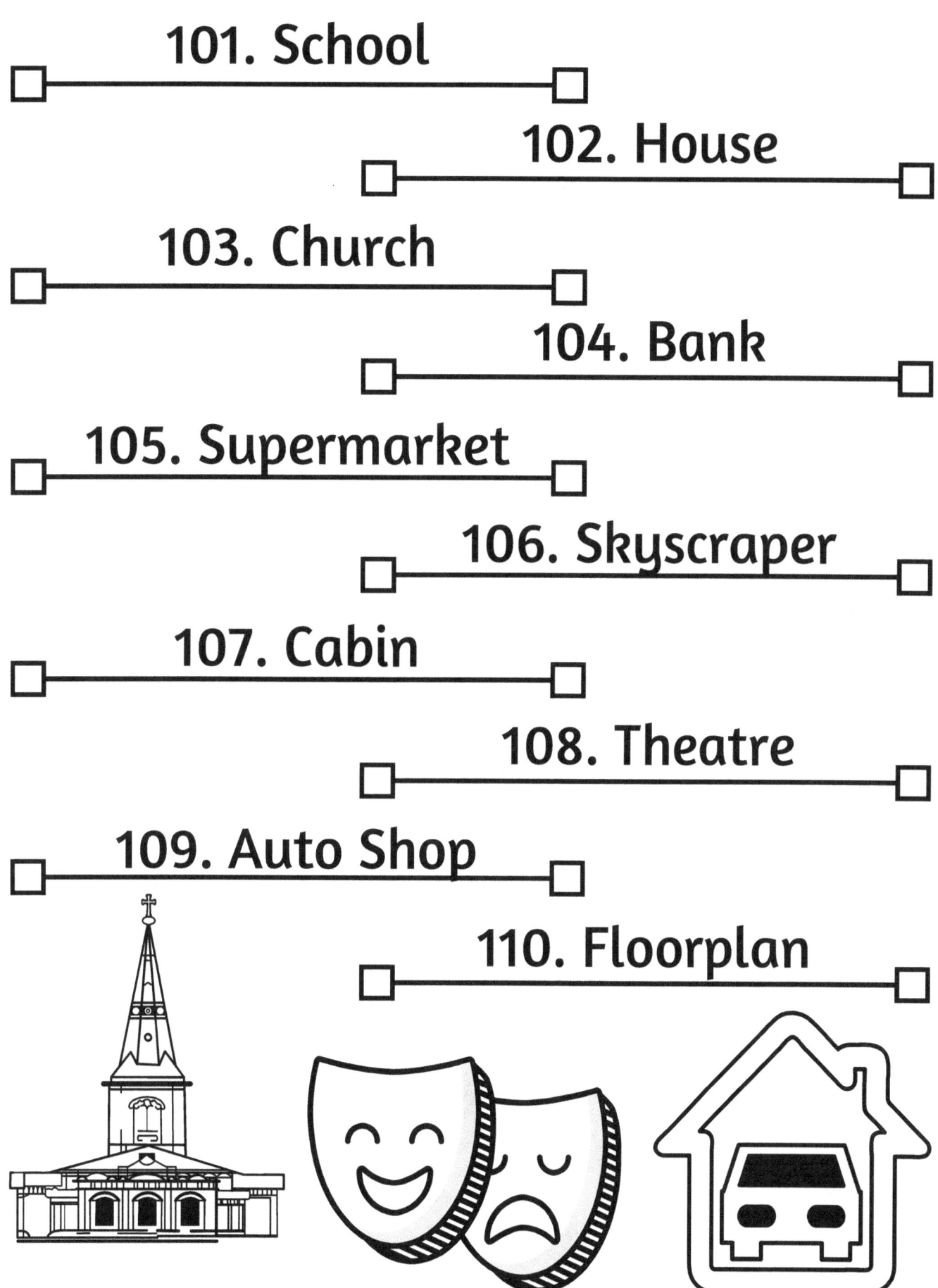

111. Sitting

112. Standing

113. Jumping

114. Laying down

115. Crawling

116. Skating

117. Dancing

118. Excited

119. Relaxing

120. Nervous

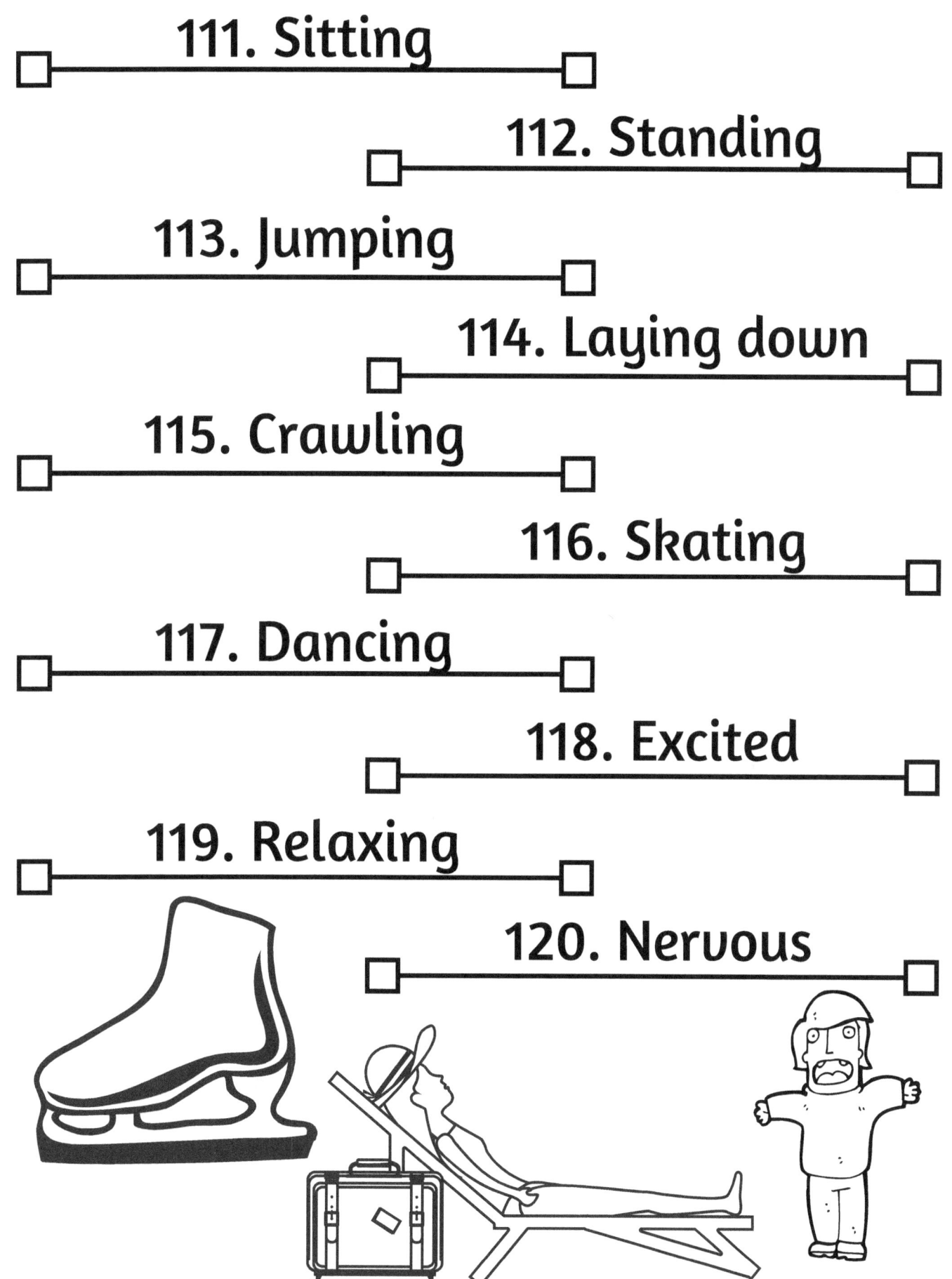

121. Shark

122. Whale

123. Dolphin

124. Sealion

125. Seahorse

126. Starfish

127. Jellyfish

128. Octopus

129. Stingray

130. Swordfish

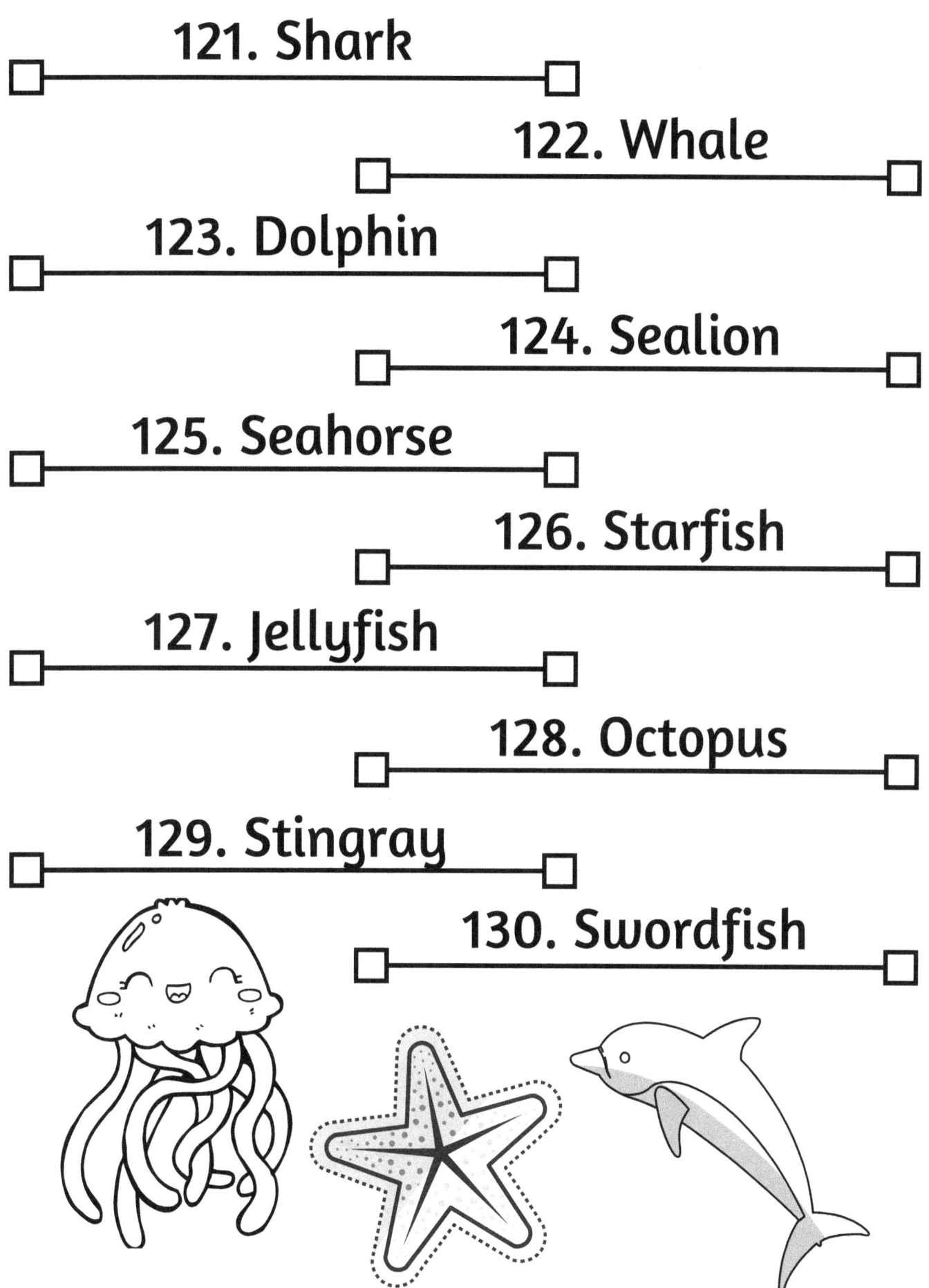

131. Lobster

132. Crab

133. Shrimp

134. Coral Reef

135. Sea anemone

136. Sea Shells

137. Ocean Waves

138. Seagull

139. Beach

140. Sandcastle

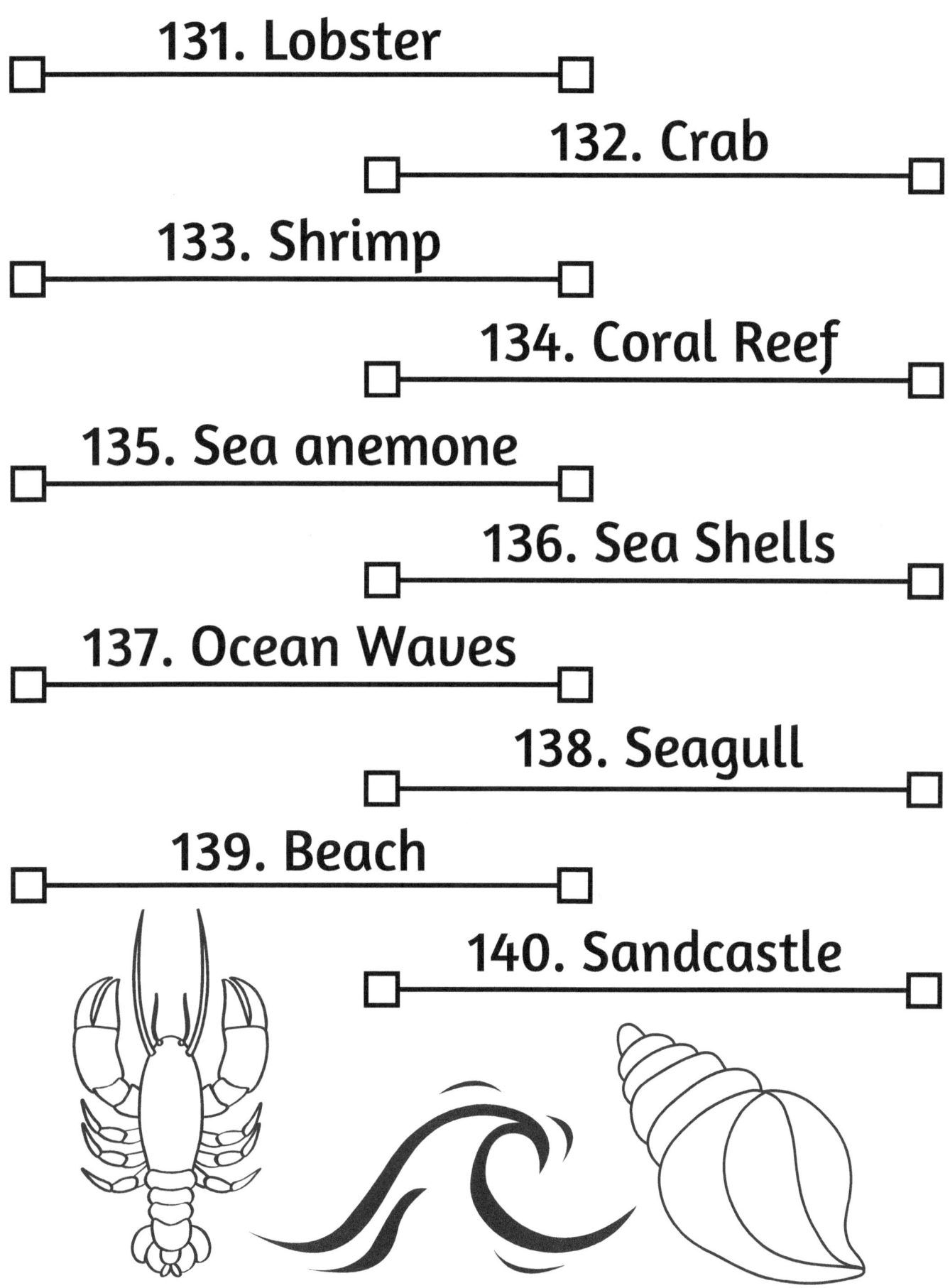

141. Snake

142. Iguana

143. Lizard

144. Gecko

145. Crocodile

146. Chameleon

147. Dinosaur

148. Turtle

149. Rabbit

150. Fox

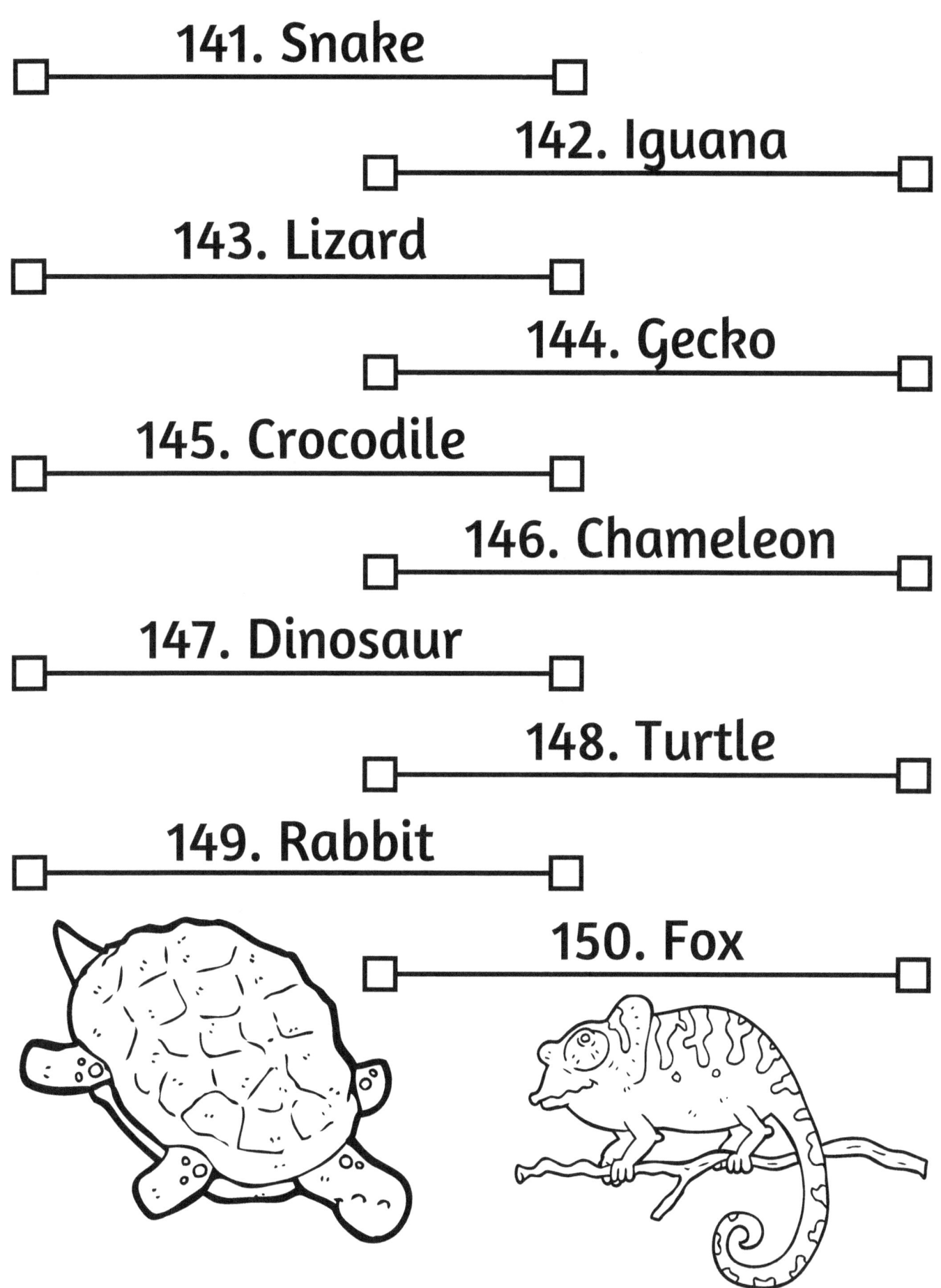

151. King

152. Queen

153. Princess

154. Prince

155. Jester

156. Throne

157. Crown

158. Castle

159. Jewels

160. Knight

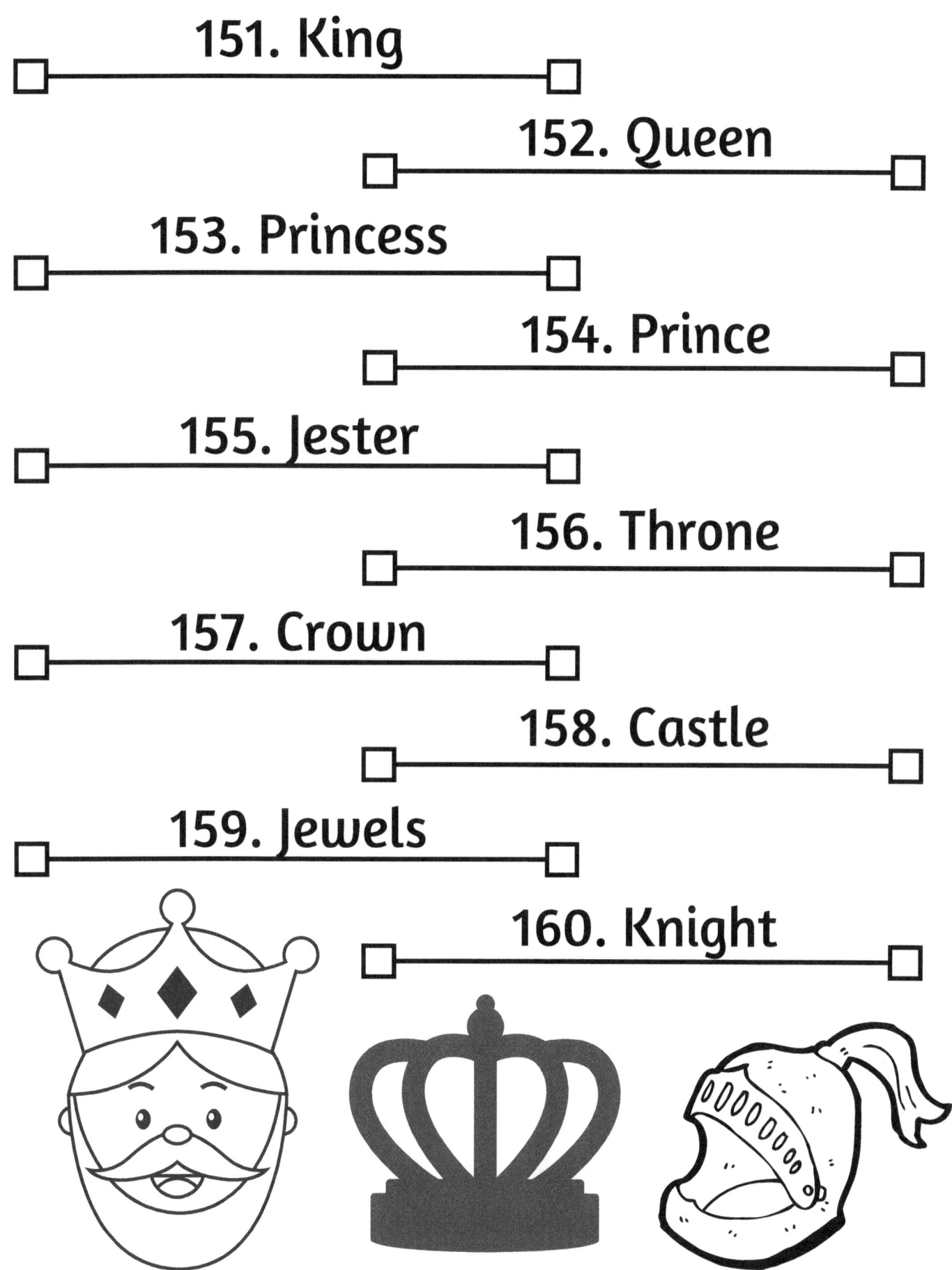

161. Doctor

162. Nurse

163. Veterinarian

164. Soldier

165. Police Officer

166. Firefighter

167. Pilot

168. Captain

169. Boy

170. Girl

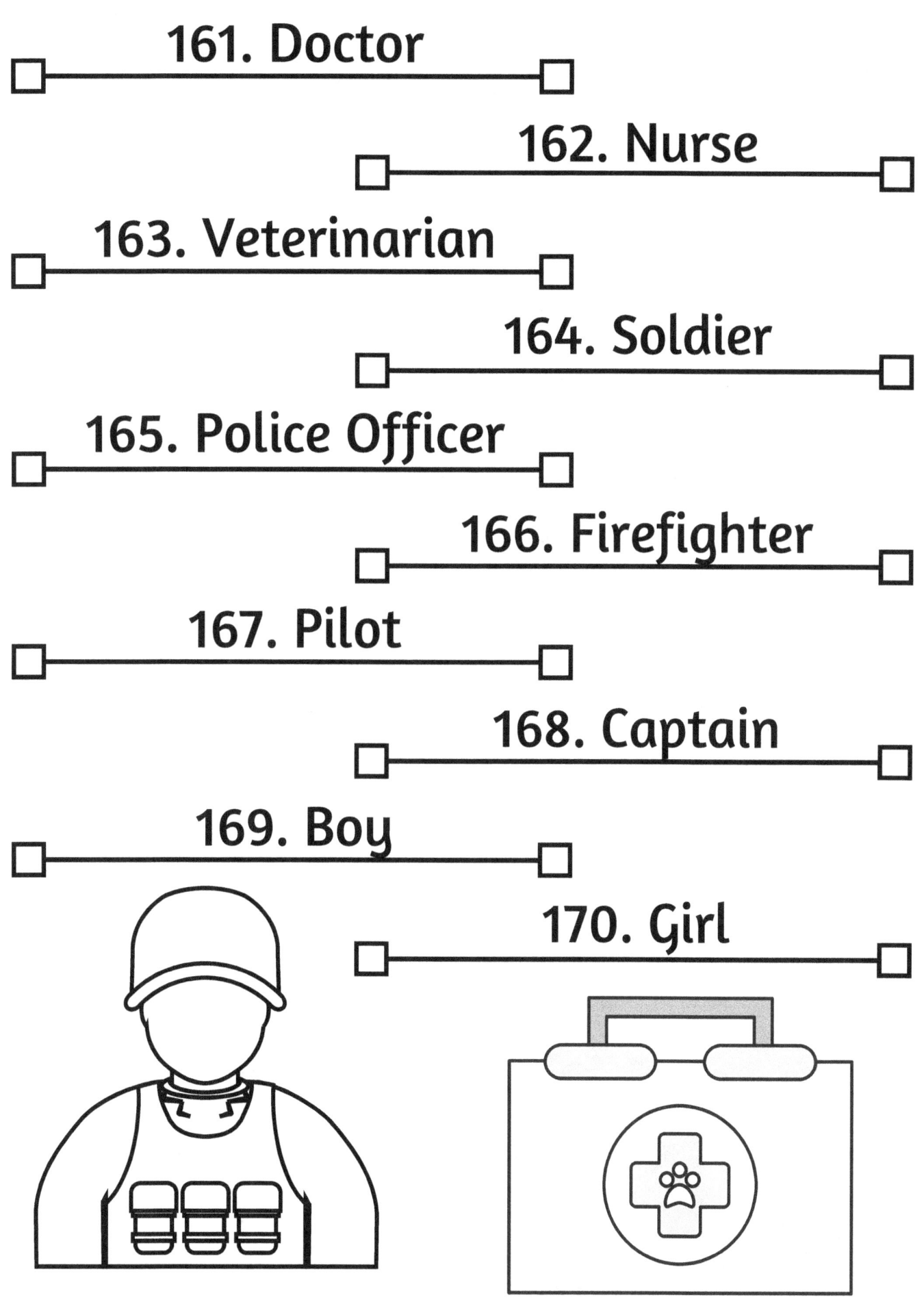

171. Pencil
172. Pen
173. Paintbrush
174. Chalk
175. Sketchbook
176. Paints
177. Markers
178. Eraser
179. Ruler
180. Crayons

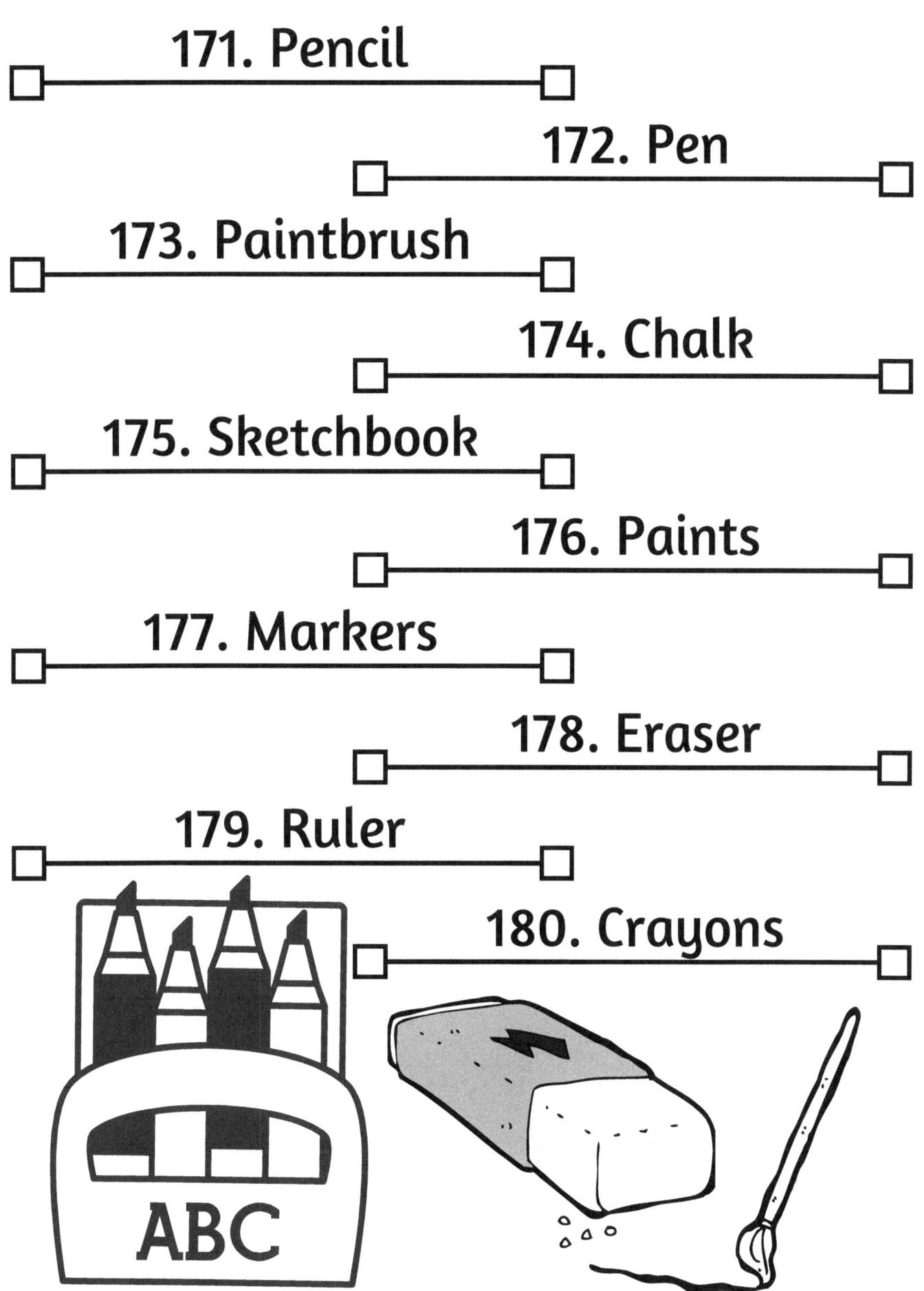

181. Pizza

182. Cheeseburger

183. Ice Cream Cone

184. Hotdog

185. Cupcake

186. Cookies

187. Donuts

188. Cherry Pie

189. Cake

190. Candy

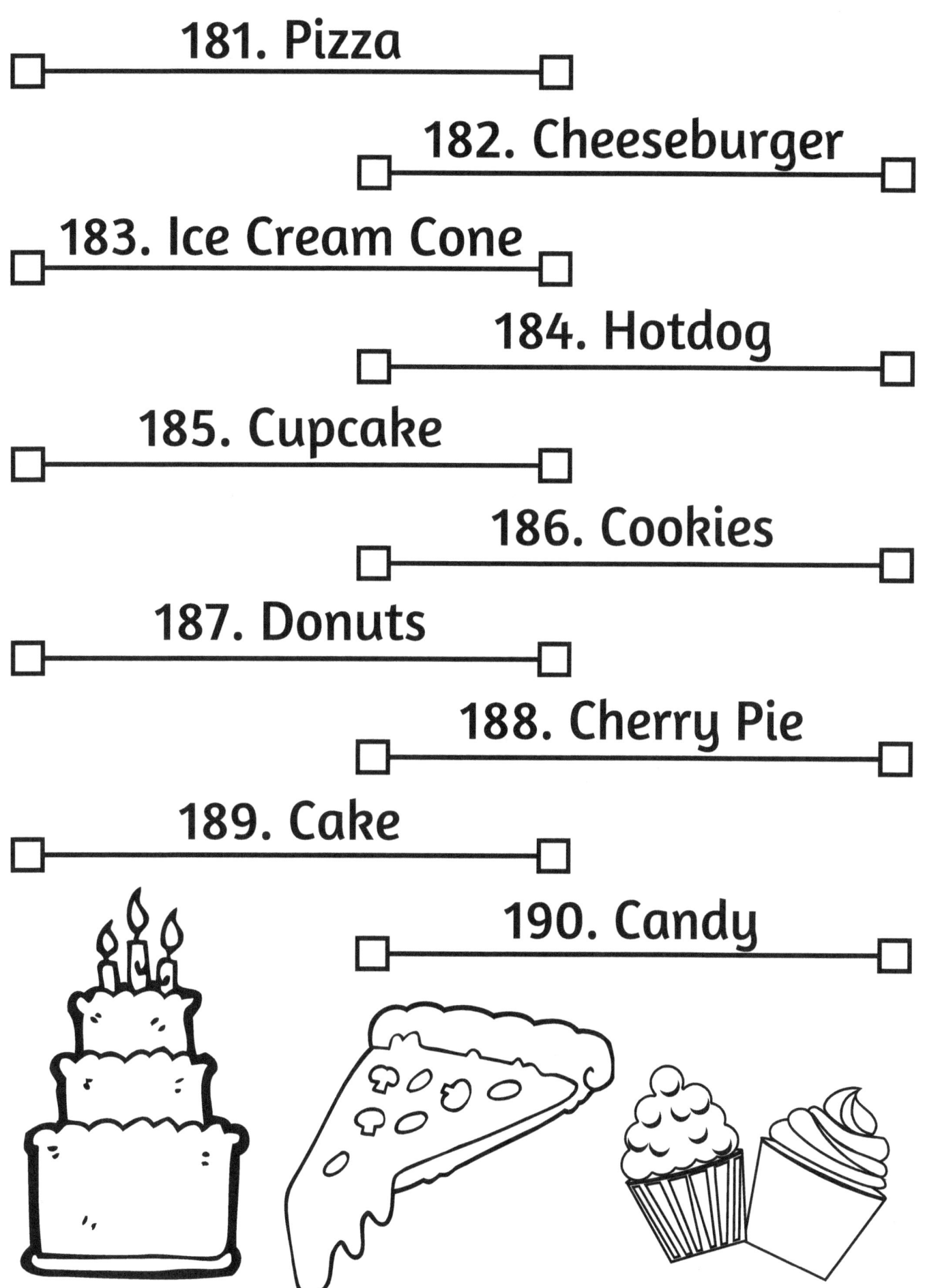

191. Sun
192. Moon
193. Clouds
194. Flowers
195. Leaf
196. Tree
197. Lightning
198. Rainbow
199. Tornado
200. Storm

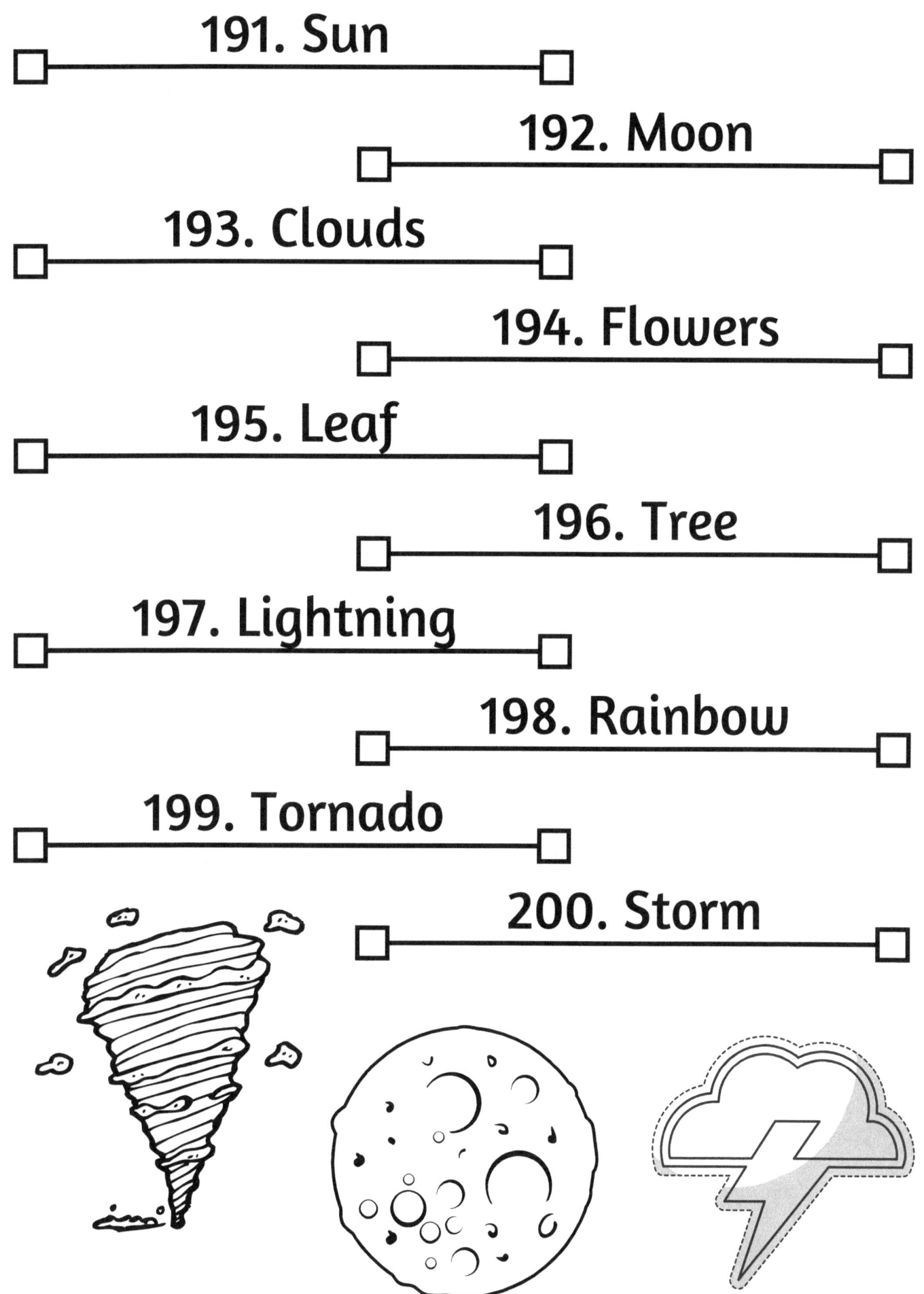

☐ 201. Pirate ☐

☐ 202. Treasure ☐

☐ 203. Pirate Ship ☐

☐ 204. Ninja ☐

☐ 205. Crystal Ball ☐

☐ 206. Superhero ☐

☐ 207. Circus ☐

☐ 208. Roller Coaster ☐

☐ 209. Ferris Wheel ☐

☐ 210. Carnival ☐

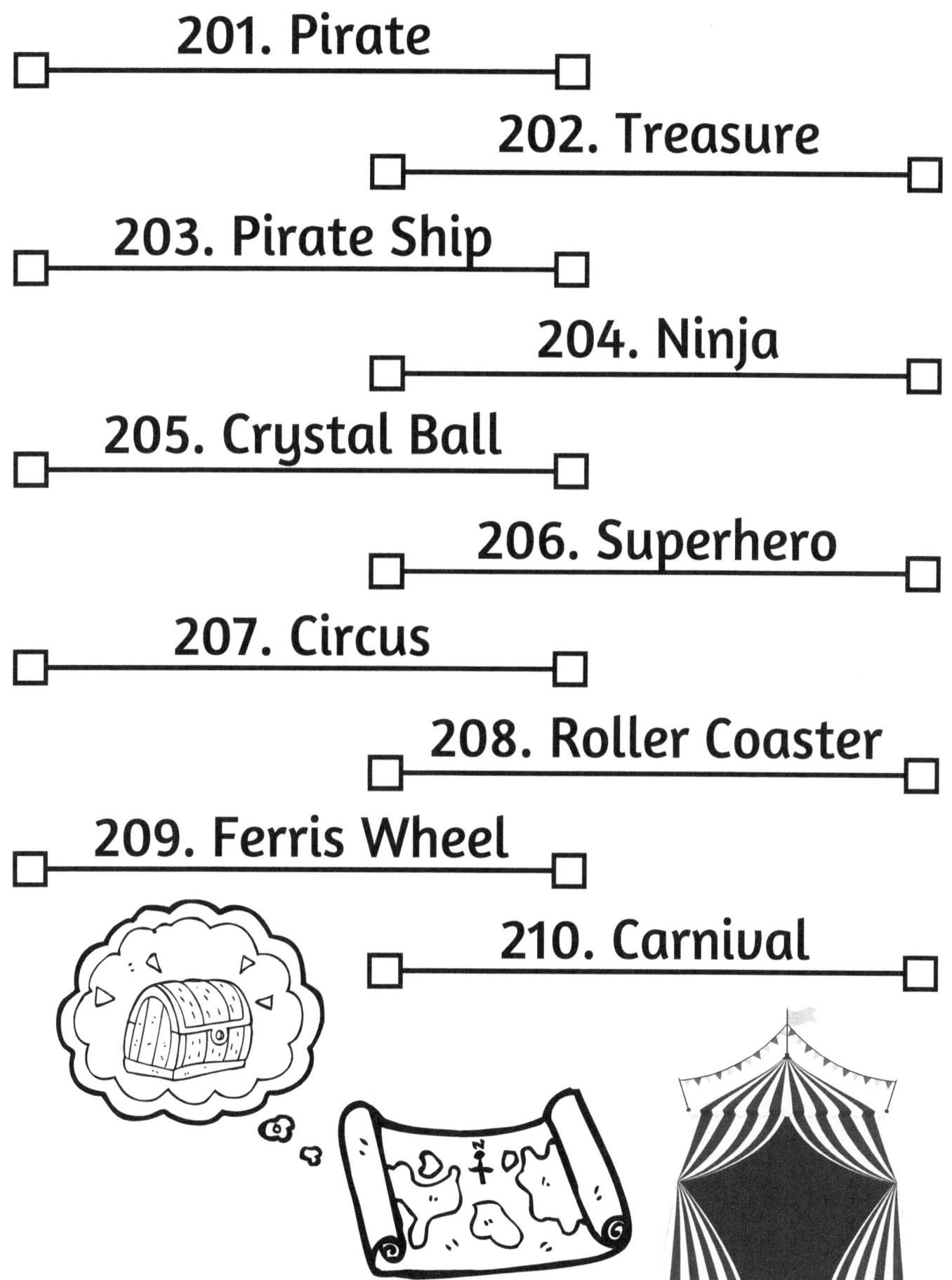

211. Toaster

212. Telephone

213. Laptop

214. Cellphone

215. Television

216. Lawnmower

217. Mailbox

218. Camera

219. Trashcan

220. Water hose

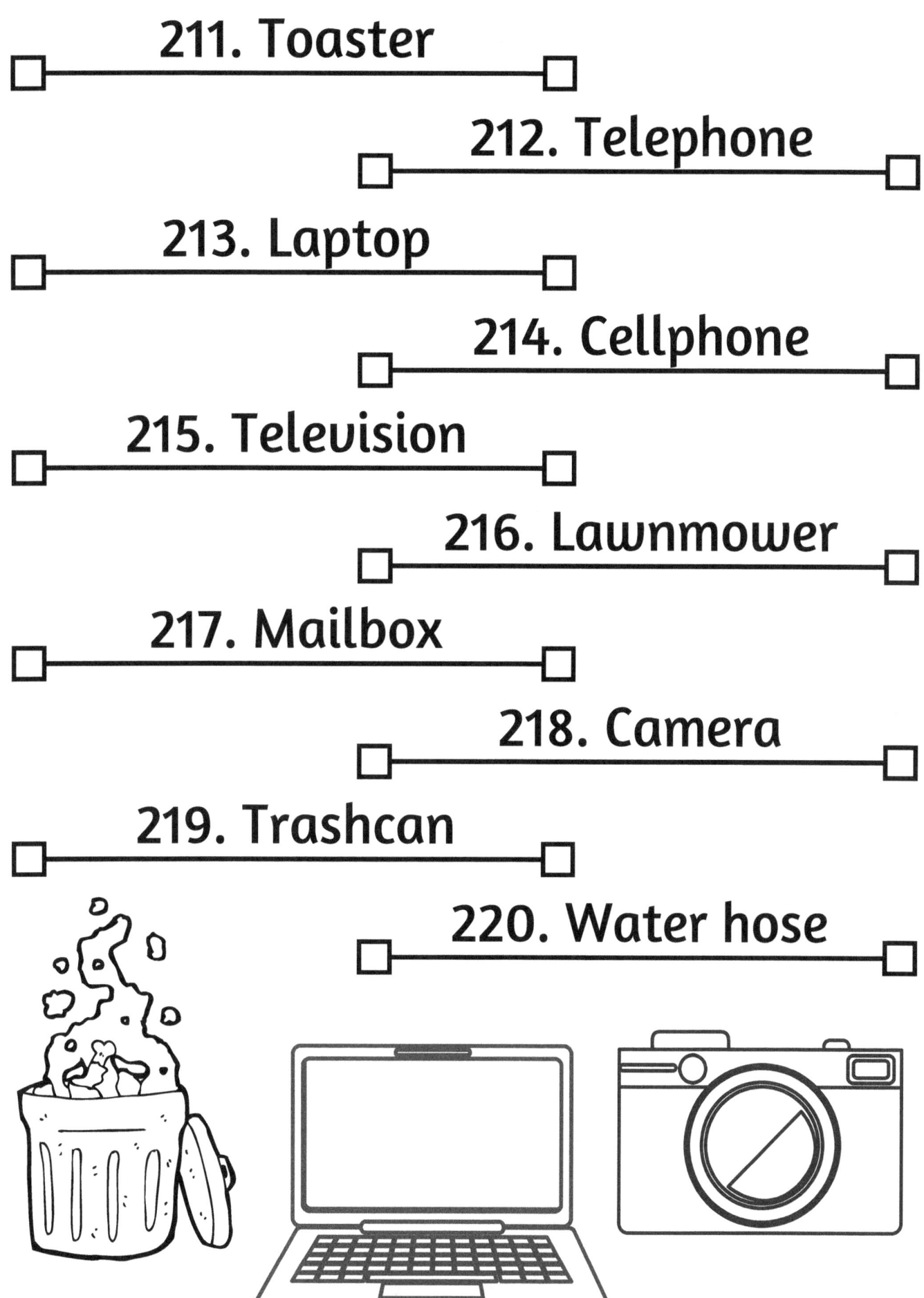

221. Milk
222. Butter
223. Bread
224. Eggs
225. Sugar
226. Popsicle
227. Salad
228. Tacos
229. Teabag
230. Spaghetti

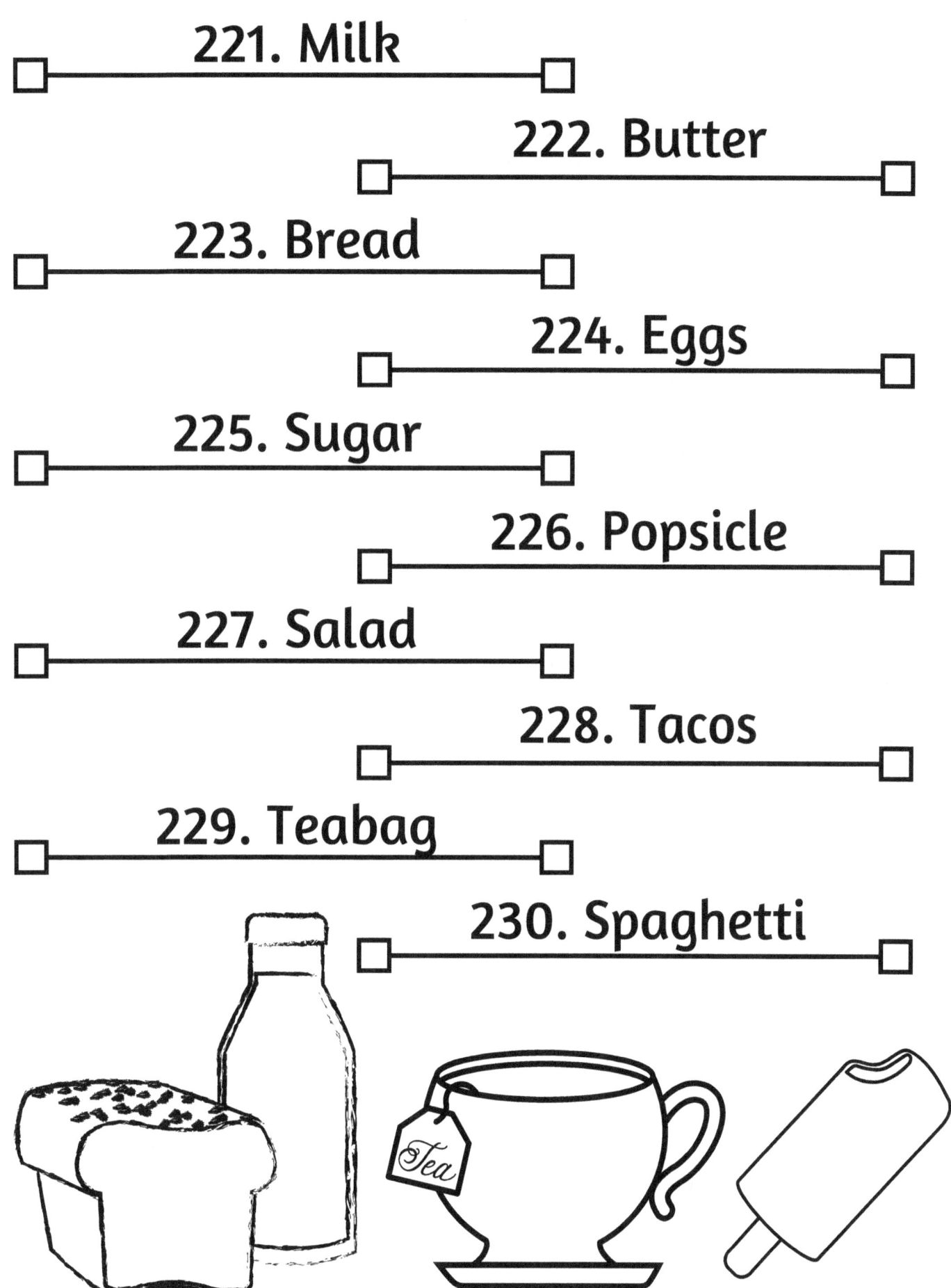

231. Garden

232. Flower bed

233. Safety Cone

234. Shed

235. Gloves

236. Flag

237. Grill

238. Pool

239. Bird Bath

240. Fire Pit

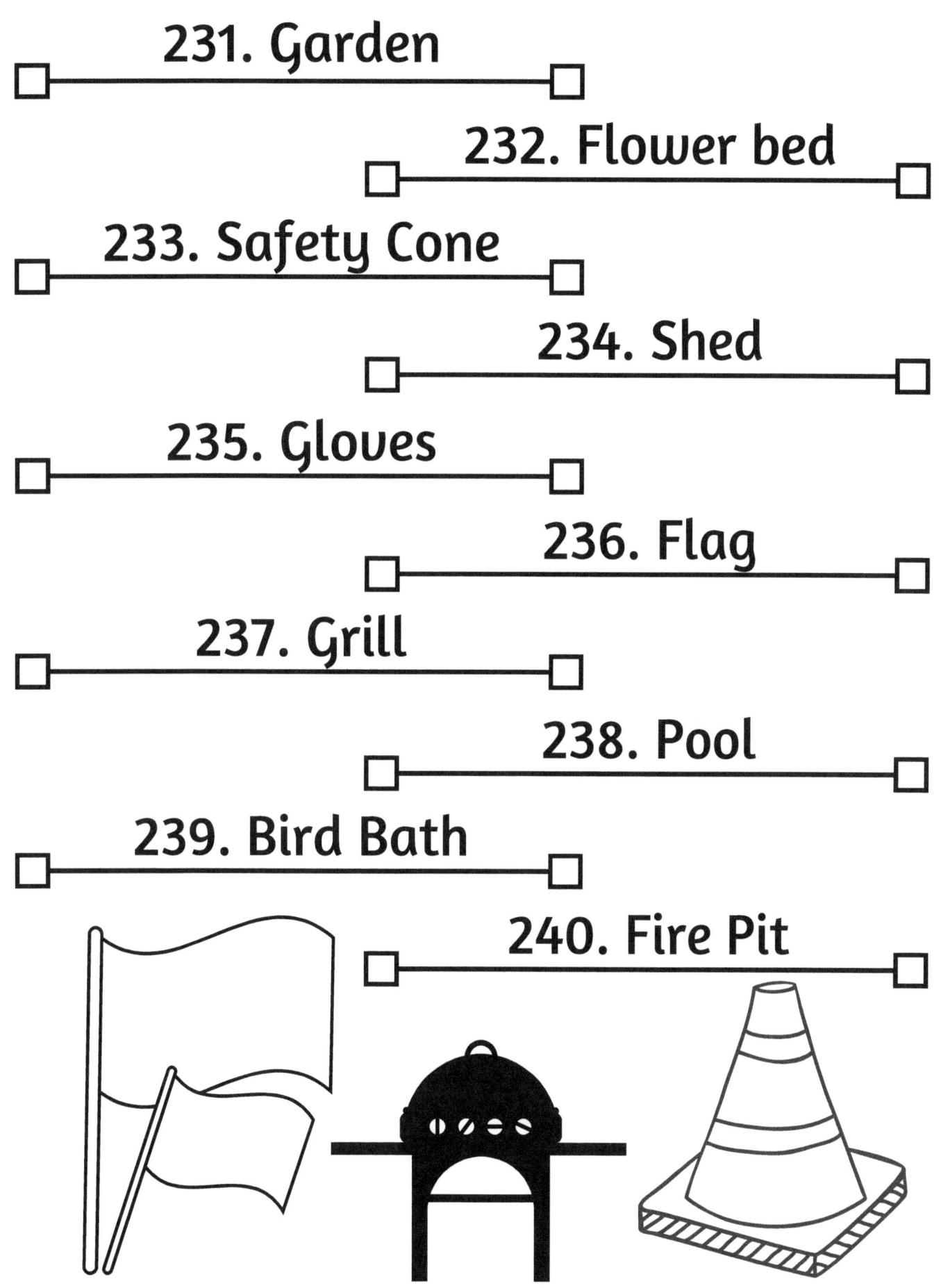

241. Mountain

242. Ocean

243. Sunset

244. Island

245. Cave

246. Volcano

247. Valley

248. Creek

249. Puddles

250. Forest

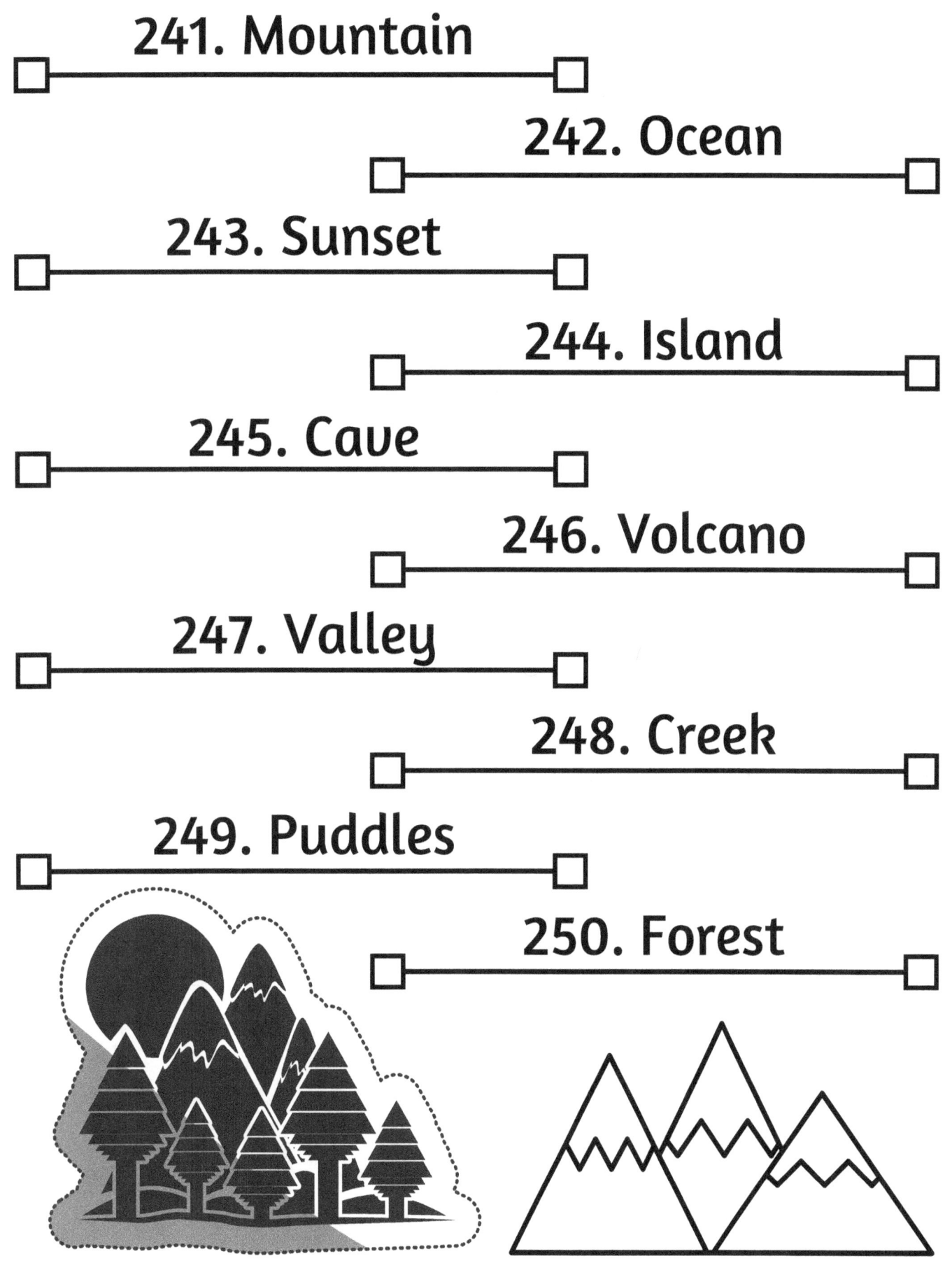

□——— 251. Hammer ———□

□——— 252. Screwdriver ———□

□——— 253. Drill ———□

□——— 254. Saw ———□

□——— 255. Rake ———□

□——— 256. Toolbox ———□

□——— 257. Wrench ———□

□——— 258. Car Jack ———□

□——— 259. Flashlight ———□

□——— 260. Hard Hat ———□

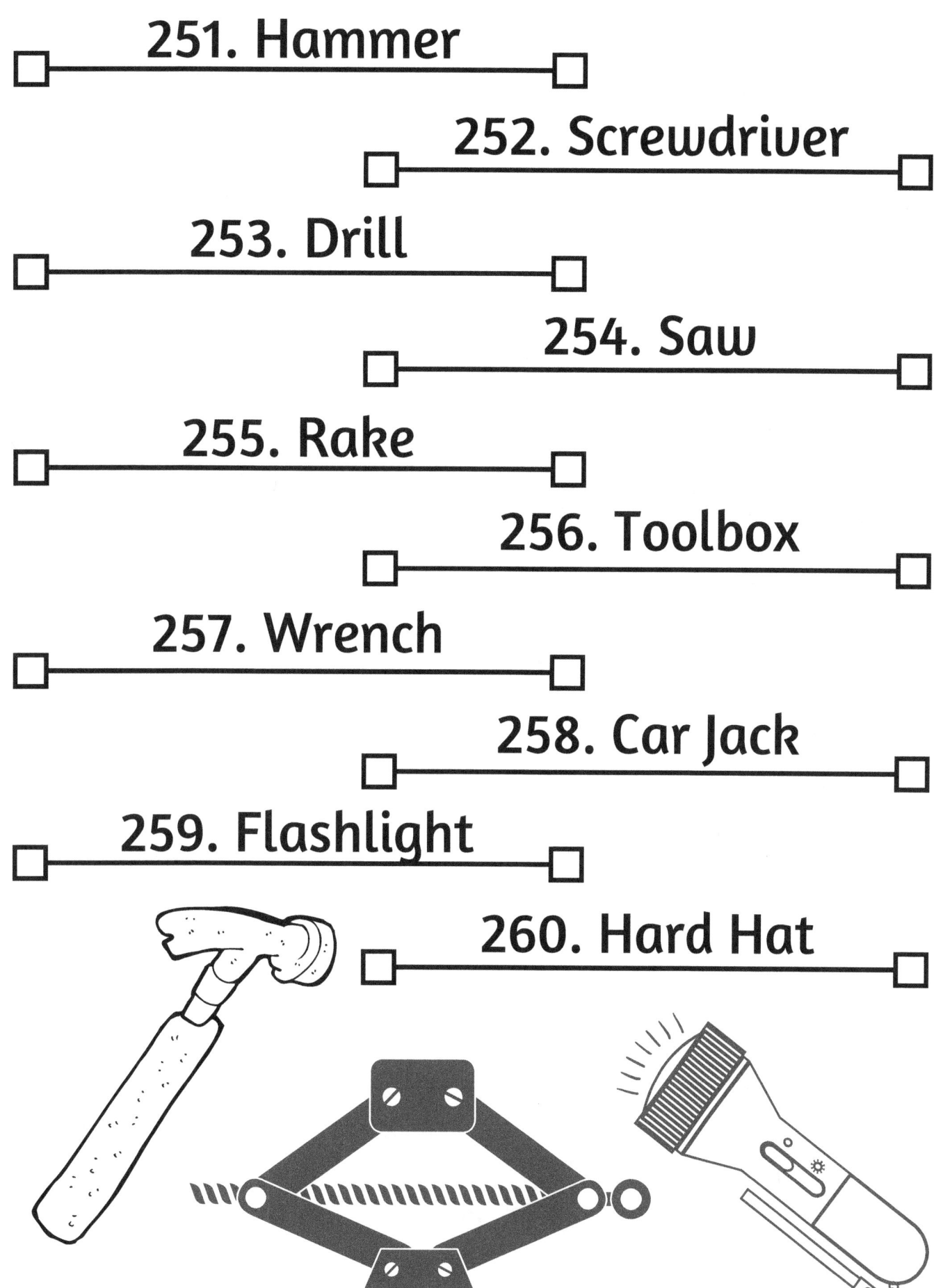

261. Concert

262. Band

263. Guitar

264. Drums

265. Microphone

266. Turntables

267. DJ Mixer

268. Speakers

269. Headphones

270. Keyboard

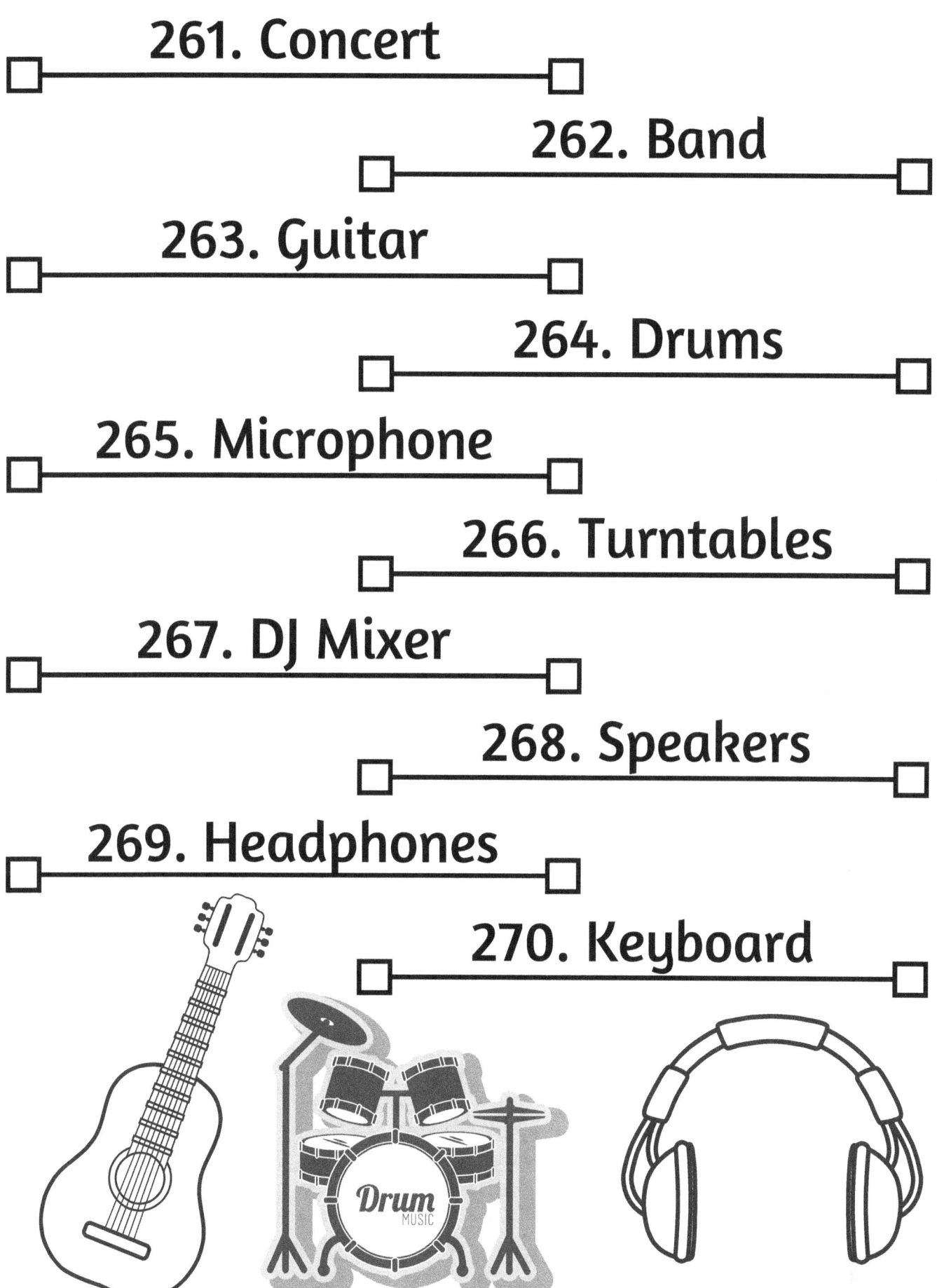

271. Fruit Basket

272. Strawberries

273. Bananas

274. Apples

275. Pineapple

276. Carrots

277. Grapes

278. Tomatoes

279. Broccoli

280. Mushrooms

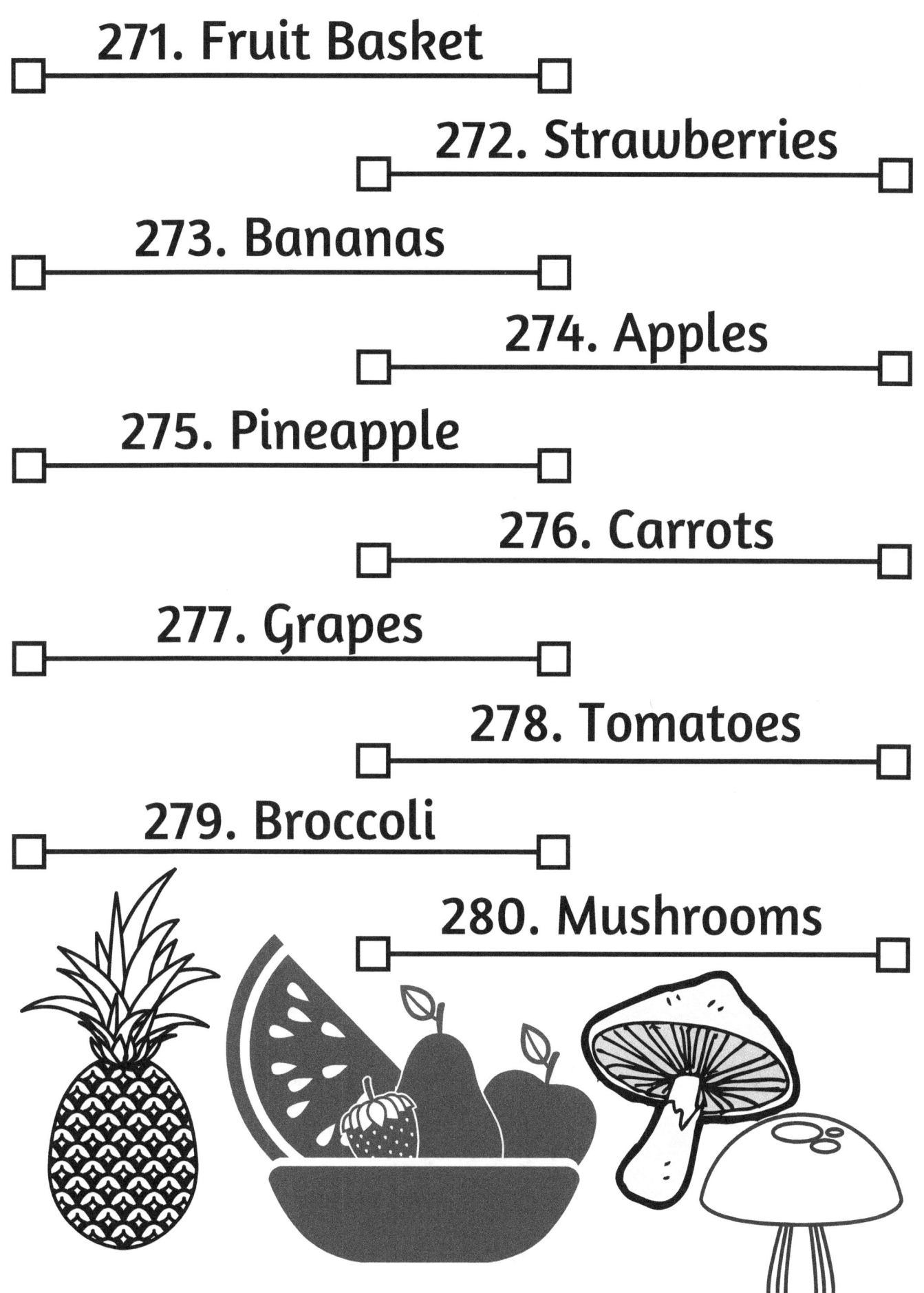

281. Skull

282. Skeleton

283. Brain

284. Heart

285. Tombstone

286. Jack-O-Lantern

287. Spider Web

288. Bat

289. Sugarskull

290. Clown

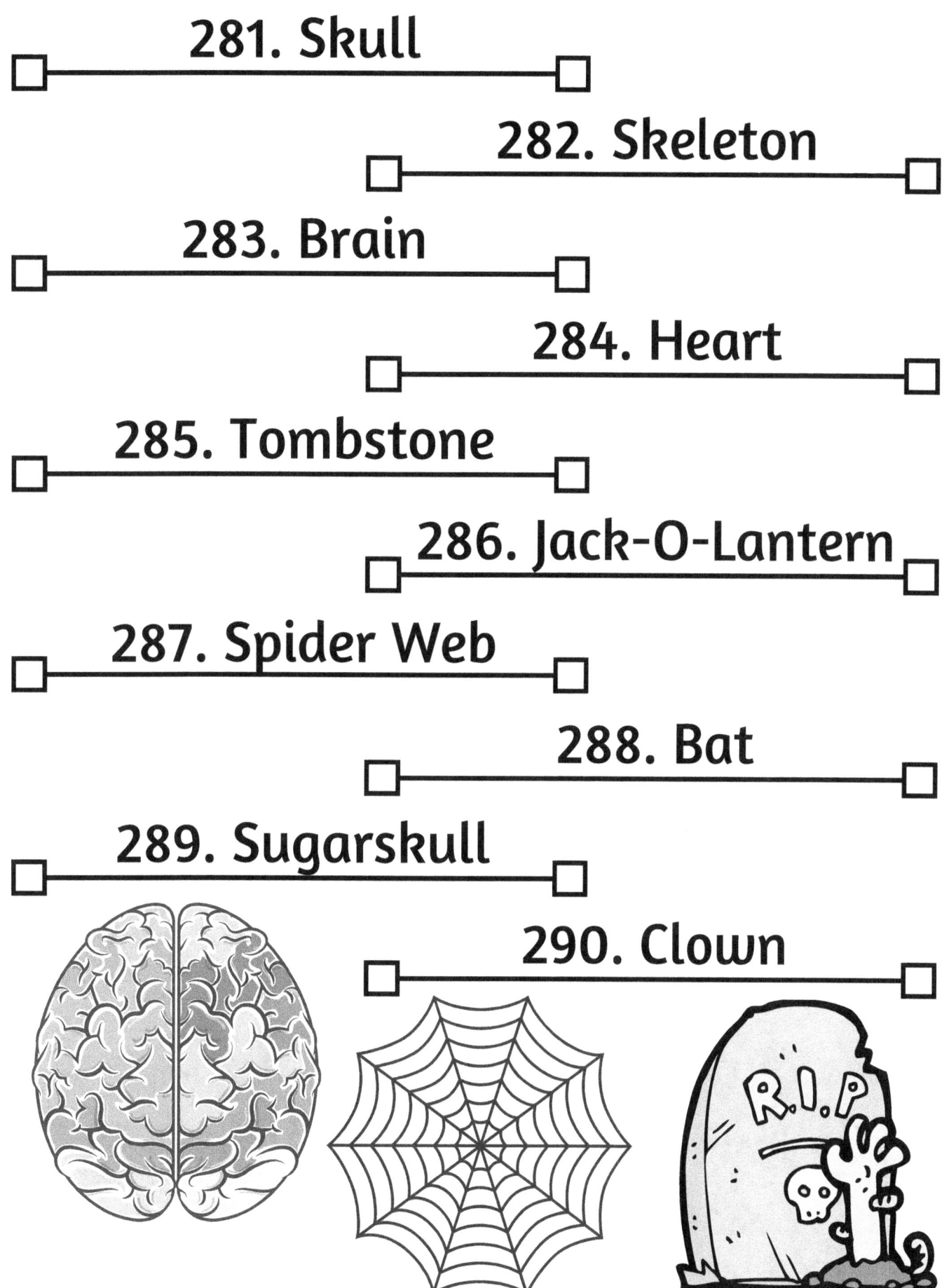

291. Party

292. Balloons

293. Candles

294. Presents

295. Streamers

296. Party Hat

297. Disco ball

298. Roller Skates

299. Skate Ramp

300. Water Slide

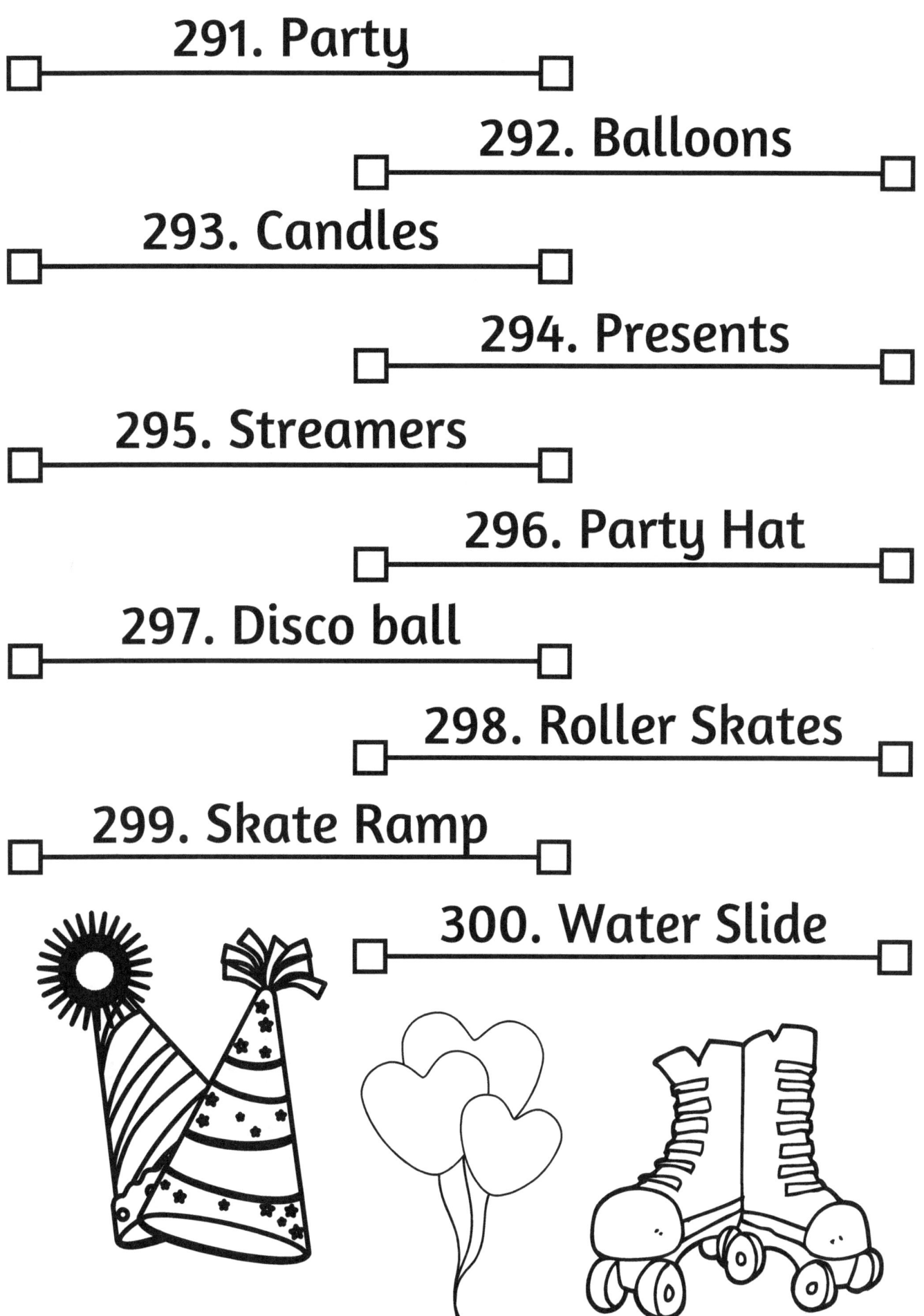

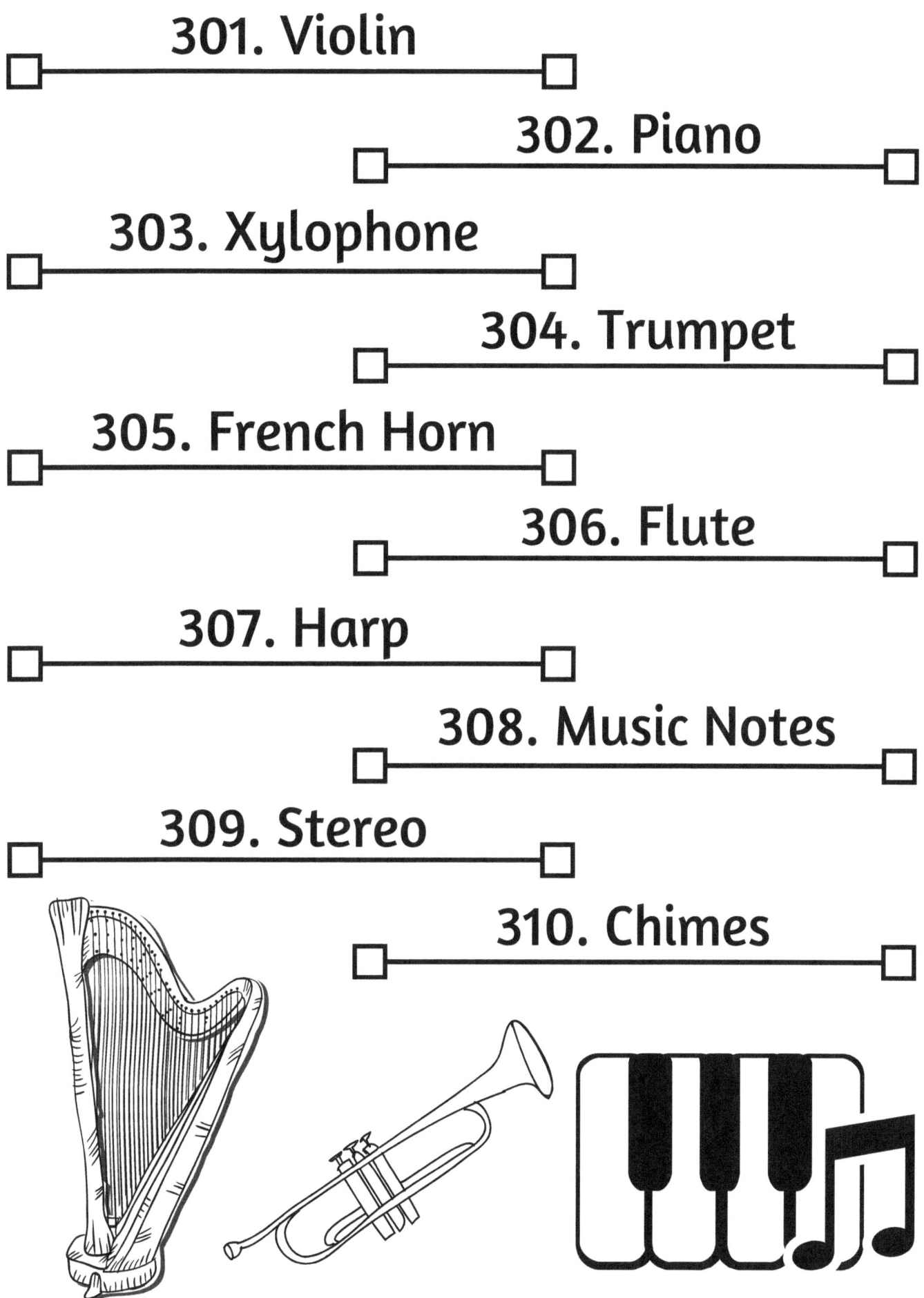

311. Snowman

312. Snowboard

313. Snowflake

314. Snowball

315. Icicle

316. Pine Tree

317. Ornament

318. Gingerbread

319. Hot Cocoa

320. Campfire

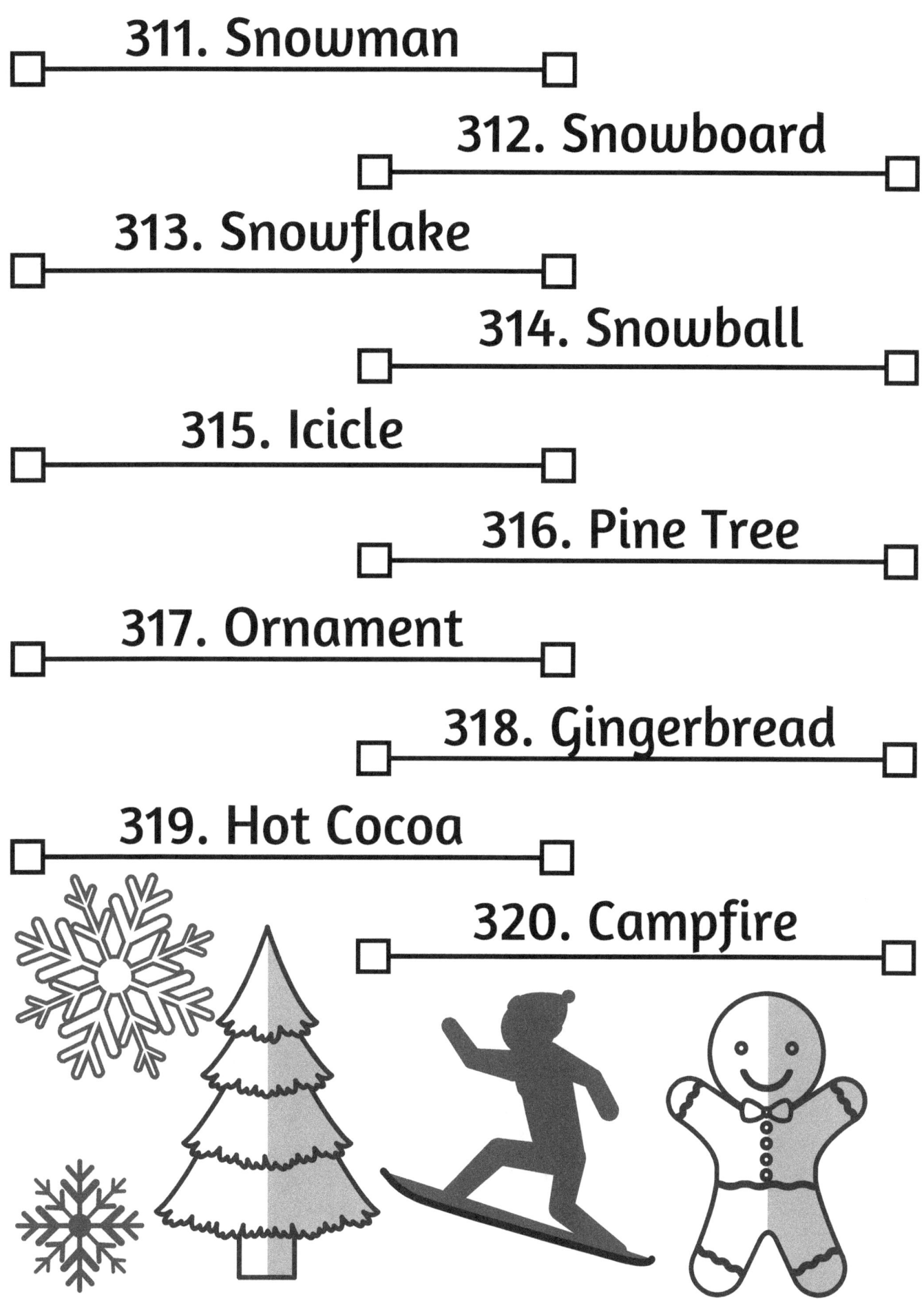

☐ 321. Jewelry box ☐

☐ 322. Necklace ☐

☐ 323. Ring ☐

☐ 324. Bracelet ☐

☐ 325. Glasses ☐

☐ 326. Gold ☐

☐ 327. Silver ☐

☐ 328. Diamonds ☐

☐ 329. Watch ☐

☐ 330. Earrings ☐

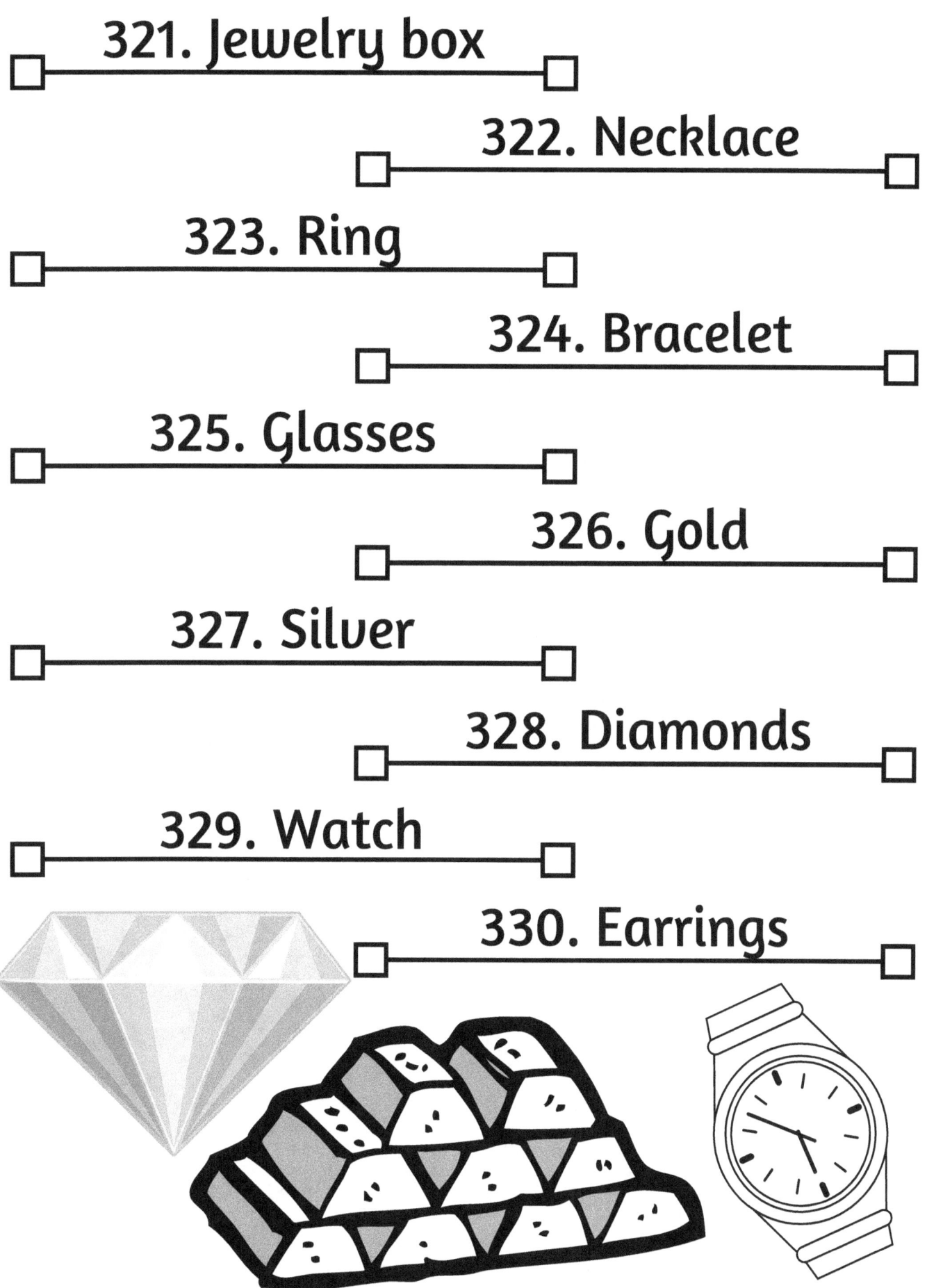

331. Mandala

332. Spirals

333. Geometric

334. Stars

335. Chevron

336. Polka Dots

337. Stripes

338. Plaid

339. Checkered

340. Paisley

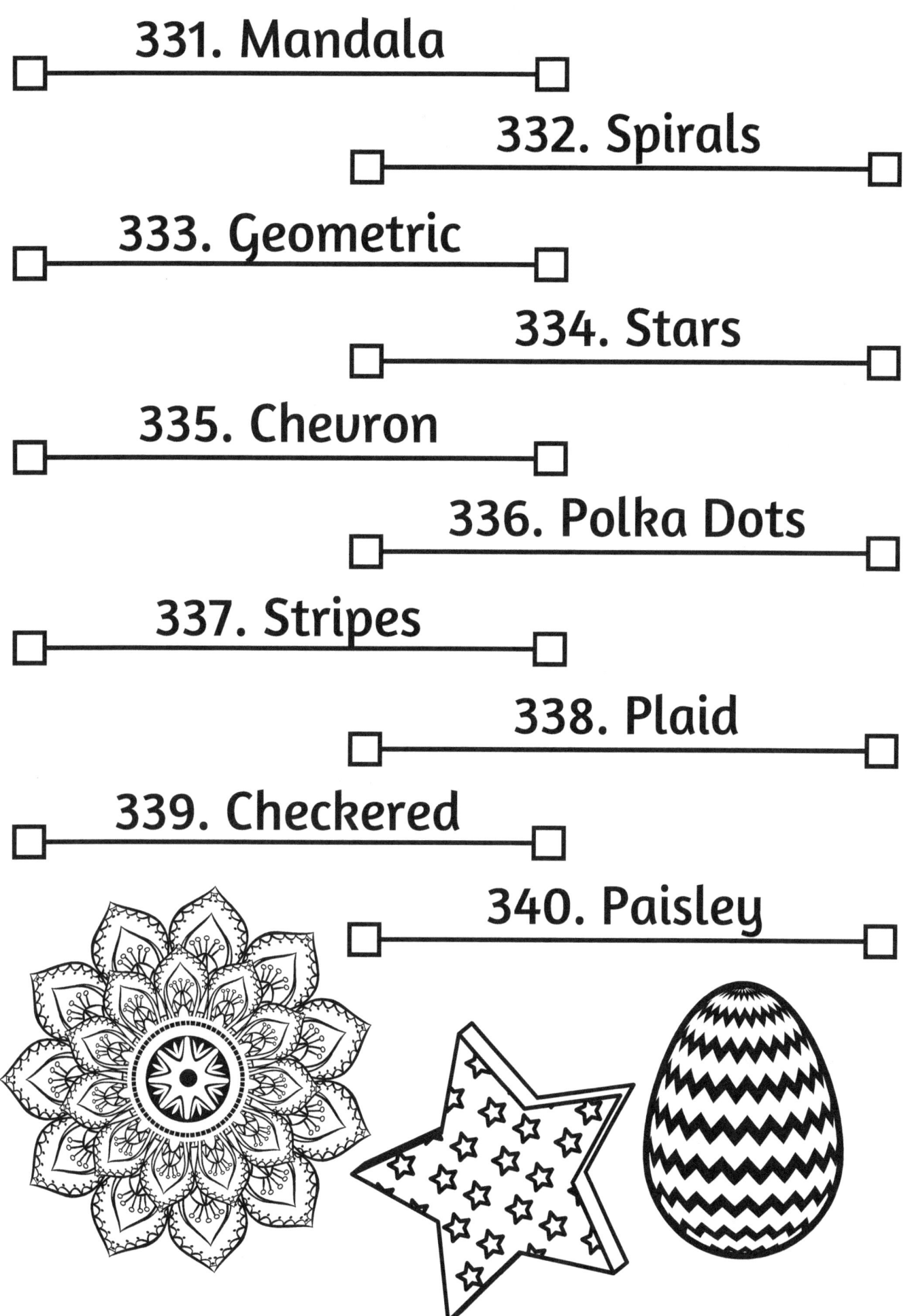

341. Dirt Bike
342. ATV
343. Racecar
344. Dune Buggy
345. Rocket
346. Astronaught
347. Spaceship
348. Alien
349. Robot
350. Gears

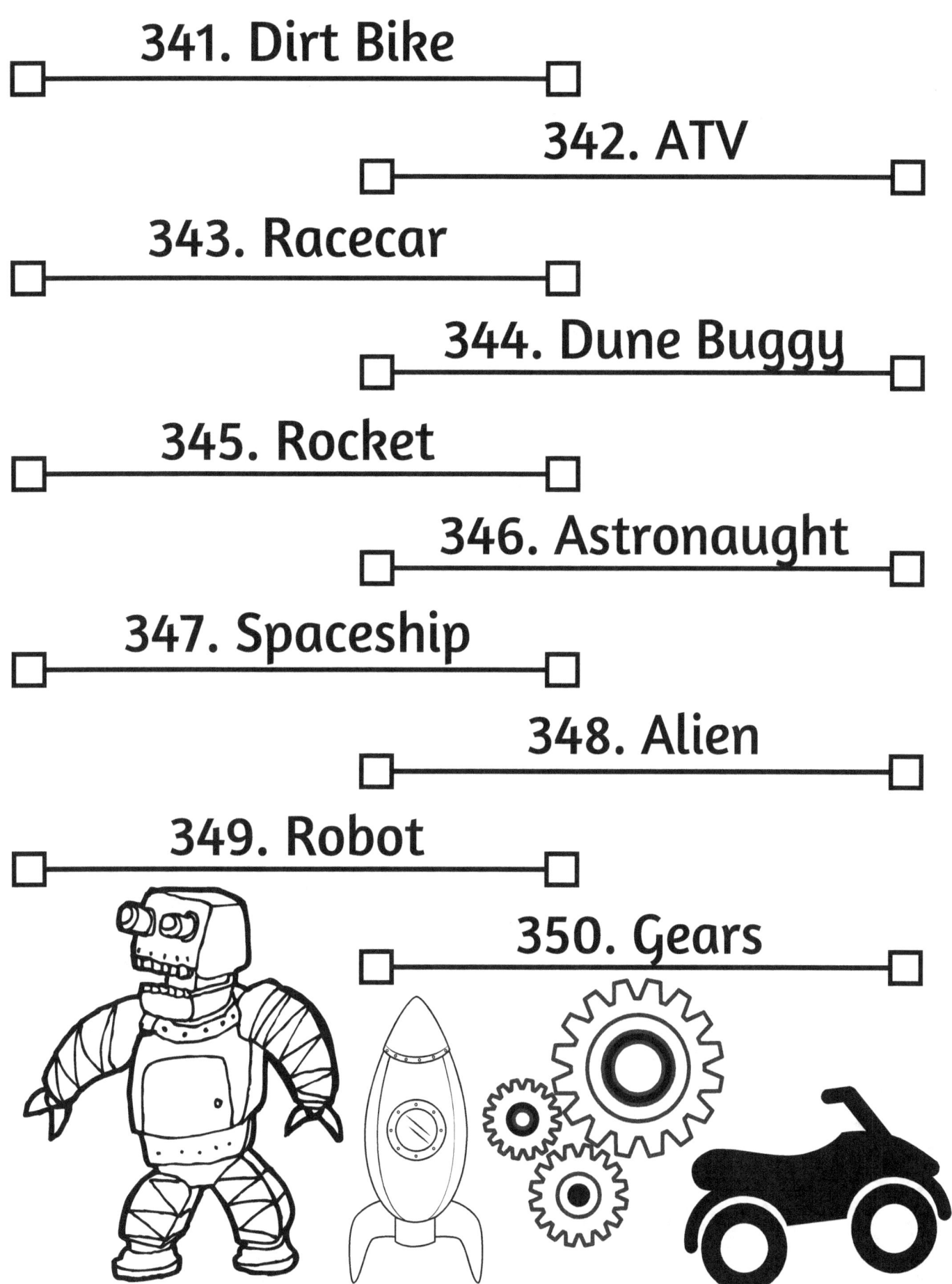

351. Ant

352. Spider

353. Butterfly

354. Caterpillar

355. Dragonfly

356. Ladybird

357. Beetle

358. Bumblebee

359. Grasshopper

360. Praying Mantis

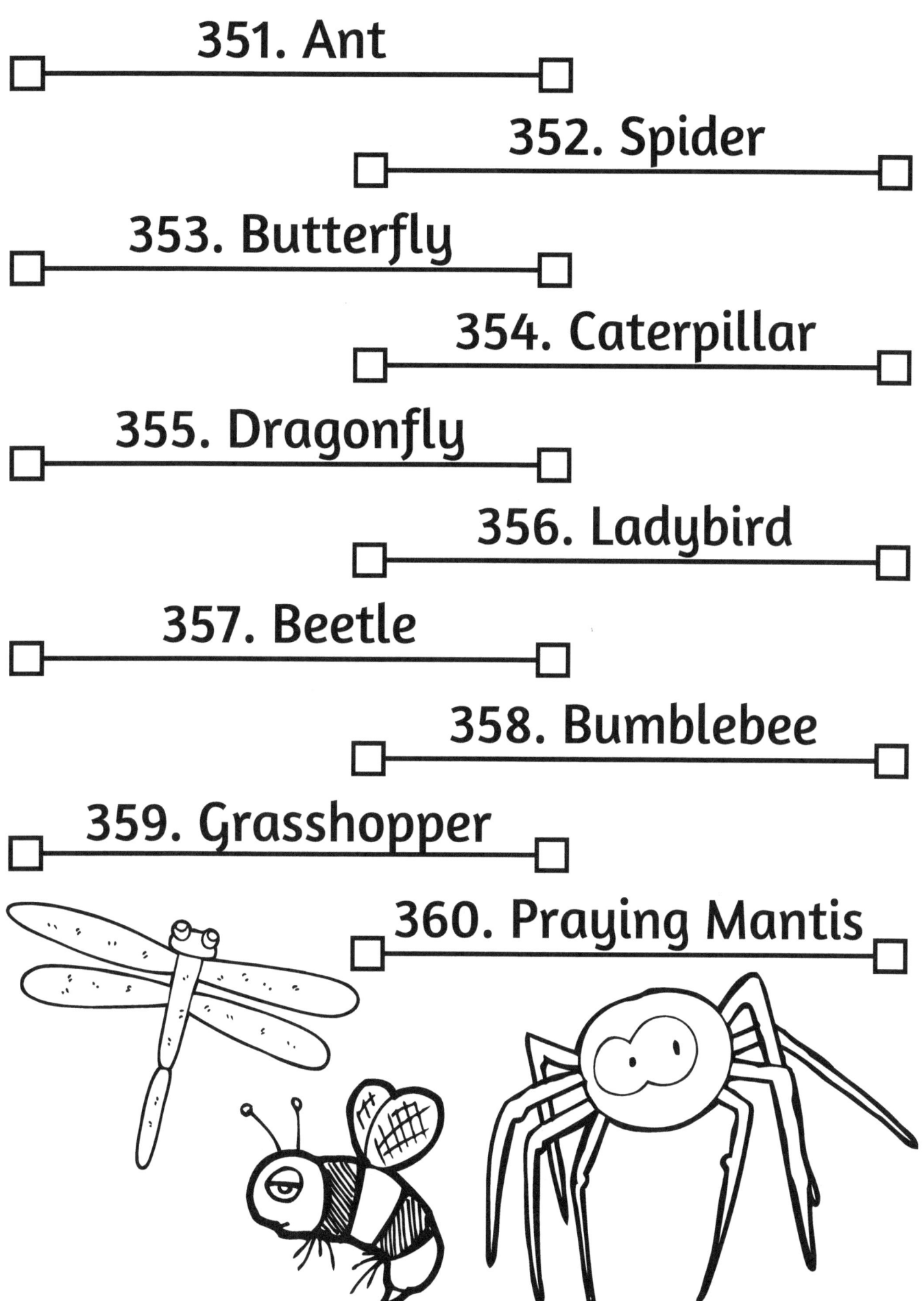

361. Cow
362. Pig
363. Chicken
364. Windmill
365. Farm

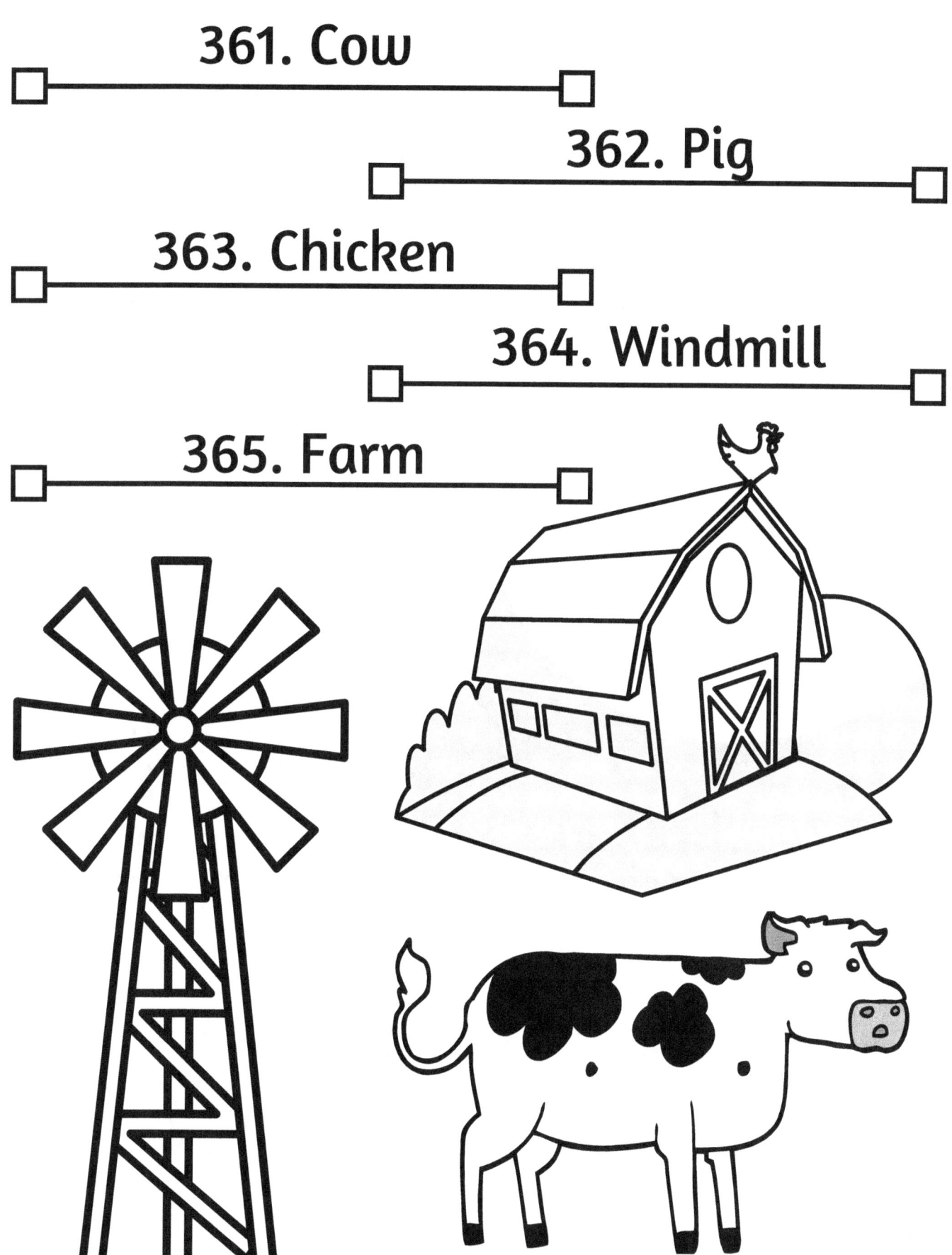

www.ingramcontent.com/pod-product-compliance
Lightning Source LLC
Chambersburg PA
CBHW081455220526
45466CB00008B/2660